DATE DUE

FE 3 00			
# 3 1 06			

DEMCO 38-296

AMERICAN POPULAR HISTORY AND CULTURE

edited by

JEROME NADELHAFT
UNIVERSITY OF MAINE

A GARLAND SERIES

"WHEN THE SPIRIT SAYS SING!"

THE ROLE OF FREEDOM SONGS IN THE CIVIL RIGHTS MOVEMENT

KERRAN L. SANGER

GARLAND PUBLISHING, INC.
NEW YORK & LONDON / 1995

ng-in-Publication Data

Sanger, Kerran L.
    "When the spirit says sing!" : the role of freedom songs in
the civil rights movement / Kerran L. Sanger.
        p.   cm. — (Garland studies in American popular history
and culture)
    Includes bibliographical references (p. 215) and index.
    ISBN 0-8153-2164-3 (alk. paper)
    1. Afro-Americans—Civil rights—Songs and music—History
and criticism. 2. Civil rights movements—United States—Songs
and music—History and criticism. 3. Protest songs—United
States—History and criticism. I. Title. II. Series.
ML3556.S26 1995
782.42'1592—dc20   95-40853

Printed on acid-free, 250-year-life paper
Manufactured in the United States of America

Contents

Preface

African-American song is one of the most resilient traditions in protest rhetoric. Since black slaves sang as a response to the conditions of slavery, African-Americans have used music and song to comment on their circumstances and to resist oppression. In spite of the centrality of song in black protest, however, relatively little scholarly work has been done to account for its incredible appeal to African Americans as a communication outlet.

Perhaps the least studied of the manifestations of black protest in song are the freedom songs of the civil rights movement. While Charles M. Payne argued that it "would be hard to overestimate the significance of the music of the movement," and several books provide the lyrics and music of the songs, the freedom songs have not received the critical attention given to, for instance, the slave spirituals.[1] Few people who were privileged to hear the songs sung at mass meetings or in jail cells were unmoved by them and, yet, little has been written that attempts to make sense of the whys and wherefores of the strong appeal of singing to the activists who sang.

This book is an extension of my doctoral thesis. As a student of rhetorical theory and criticism, my interest is in better understanding public persuasion and the means by which people communicate, in purposeful ways, with others. Motivated by an interest in the masses who make up mass movements, as opposed to the leaders, I was moved by what I had heard and read about the civil rights movement and intrigued by the repeated references to the role of singing in that movement. I had been taught to be curious about the symbolic choices people make in their attempts to communicate with others. Although, in retrospect, singing seems an obvious choice for the civil rights activists, I knew that they were faced with many rhetorical possibilities, that they consciously discussed the value of different strategies, and out of this consideration singing, and certain songs, became featured choices. Why? What did singing offer that could not be achieved by more traditional forms of public discourse? Such questions are at the heart of this study.

The research methods of most rhetorical critics are primarily qualitative. This study relies on several such methods and, while the focus of the book will be on findings not on method, a few words about the research approaches may be useful. One approach I used was the exploration of implicit communication or rhetorical theory. A study of implicit rhetorical theory is a study of the generalizations people make regarding the nature of communication, generalizations that do not constitute a formal or explicit theory but that lead people to depict communication to others in certain ways and may guide communication choices. Thomas W. Benson defined the study of implicit communication theories, saying:

> implicit communication theory refers to the collection of ideas that lay practitioners hold about the way they and others communicate. Such ideas are theoretical because they relate to one another and to generalized views of the world.[2]

Such implicit claims held by lay practitioners compose an attitude toward communication that affects their choice of rhetorical strategies and may lead them to respond in certain ways to such strategies.

Henry Louis Gates, Jr., has worked in similar directions and has sought to articulate an implicit "theory of reading that is there, that has been generated from within the black tradition itself."[3] His work regarding implicit theories of black tradition can be added to the work of rhetorical critics studying implicit rhetorical theories, and applied to the question of the power of music and song in the lives of African Americans.

In my analysis, I explored the ways African Americans described for themselves the role of song as a communication strategy in their protests. I examined how the song leaders and activists of the civil rights movement described the singing of their freedom songs, and how they depicted singing as providing specific rhetorical opportunities for them that they perceived to be less attainable via other communication outlets. The text for this portion of the analysis was not the actual freedom songs but, rather, what activists said about the songs as a form of communication in a crucial phase of black protest. Black testimony about the power of song is especially accessible from the era of the civil rights movement in the United States, with many activists commenting on the prevalence of song in that movement.[4]

The analysis of the implicit rhetorical theory of civil rights activists as it emerged from their testimony regarding the movement provided insight to the characteristics of African American communication traditions, and a sense of what African Americans considered to be most important to their persuasive success during the civil rights era. The analysis indicated that many civil rights activists glorified song, and privileged it as a powerful and effective form of expression rivaling speech and other rhetorical acts as a means of accomplishing their goals. In their comments, activists made apparent their conviction that certain specific characteristics of singing contributed to its power and appeal.

The study of implicit rhetorical theory also helps ensure that the discourse of a group, in this case the discourse of black activists for civil rights, is analyzed and evaluated, not by traditional Eurocentric standards of rhetorical excellence, but by standards that account for the characteristic style of the group. Gates, for one, has argued for the need to fully appreciate black literary and rhetorical expressions without depending on "literary theories borrowed from other traditions."[5] The use of the study of implicit rhetorical theory encourages us to consider the songs and music of black tradition with an eye to understanding what the singers felt was so valuable about this form of communication in African American protest.

In addition to the investigation into the implicit rhetorical theory of civil rights activists, I have also engaged in close textual analysis of the lyrics of the freedom songs. This method consisted of careful analysis of the words of the songs, with special attention given to patterns of language use, such as the use of personal pronouns, the use of words describing activists and other "players" in the movement, metaphors and other language devices that set the songs off from everyday talk, and so on. The analysis of such communication features provided insight to what it was about the songs that generated persuasive appeal.

The textual analysis was also grounded in the tradition of work done by Laura Crowell and Jill Taft-Kaufman.[6] Their work can be called the study of "rhetorical evolution," the ways that a message is changed in the stages of its creation. Many of the songs sung during the civil rights movement were adapted from much older songs in the folk tradition, and it is informative to analyze the changes made in the lyrics as the songs were pressed into service in the civil rights movement.

Civil rights activists, in choosing songs to sing, concocted an intriguing blend of old and new. They could have, and in some cases did, craft entirely new songs to serve the special needs of the movement. Generally, however, they eschewed this option, instead choosing to sing songs that had been in the black singing tradition, or in other protest traditions, for many years. Though activists were drawn to the old songs, they often introduced their own, sometimes extensive, changes in those songs. By recognizing these changes, and also by looking carefully at what activists chose to preserve from the old songs, we are provided with a valuable look at the ways a group of people managed language to accomplish their purposes.

As a means of getting at the strategic choices made in adapting traditional songs to a modern movement, a two-level analysis was used. A number of songs were compared, first, with their own traditional origins and, second, with one another as they were sung by civil rights activists. This analysis demonstrated the kinds of changes the songs underwent, providing insight to modifications made and the ways those modifications contributed to the persuasive message of the civil rights movement.

I focused my analysis primarily on songs that were adapted from black singing tradition, rather than songs that were specifically written for the movement. These songs were mentioned often in the testimony of the activists, and in books and published reports about the movement, and they seem to have made up the core of the repertoire of songs sung most often during movement activities. The full texts of songs referred to in the book appear in the appendix. The appendix also includes details about the genesis of the songs and the evolution of the songs prior to and during the civil rights movement. It should be noted that, although song texts are provided and my analysis was based primarily on those texts, the freedom songs were not fixed in content. It was customary for activists to add relevant verses to the songs extemporaneously, so the songs varied a great deal. My sense is, however, that the lyrics that found their way into print were the best-loved lyrics that remained constant, while other verses were added and deleted.

Many people supported my work. Thomas Benson, Richard Gregg, and Dennis Gouran of the Speech Communication Department, and Caroline Eckhardt of the Comparative Literature Department, at Penn State University, comprised my doctoral committee. They provided feedback and motivation at crucial stages of the writing of the dissertation from which this book grew. The Chair of the Communication Department, Emile Netzhammer, and the Acting Dean of Arts and Humanities, Dennis McCarthy, at Buffalo State College, provided support and resources. My family, especially my husband, Don Turner, and my mother, Evelyn Sanger, have exhibited great patience, and have always believed in the value of this work. My sincere thanks to all.

NOTES

1. Charles M. Payne, *I've Got the Light of Freedom: The Organizing Tradition and the Mississippi Freedom Struggle* (Berkeley: University of California Press, 1995), 261. The following are excellent sources of the words and music of the freedom songs: Guy Carawan and Candie Carawan, *We Shall Overcome!: Songs of the Southern Freedom Movement* (New York: Oak, 1963); Guy Carawan and Candie Carawan, *Freedom Is a Constant Struggle: Songs of the Freedom Movement* (New York: Oak, 1968); Pete Seeger and Bob Reiser, *Everybody Says Freedom* (New York: W.W. Norton, 1989). For additional rhetorical analysis of the freedom songs, see G. Jack Gravlee, "A Black Rhetoric of Social Revolution," in *A New Diversity in Contemporary Southern Rhetoric*, ed. Calvin M. Logue and Howard Dorgan (Baton Rouge: Louisiana State University Press, 1987), 52-88. Bernice Johnson Reagon, a civil rights leader and former member of the Freedom Singers, has written a good deal on the subject as well. See Bernice Johnson Reagon, "In Our Hands: Thoughts on Black Music," *Sing Out!* November 1975, 1-2, 5; Bernice Johnson Reagon, "Songs of the Civil Rights Movement 1955-1965: A Study in Culture History," (Ph.D. diss., Howard University, 1975); Bernice Johnson Reagon, booklet accompanying three phonodiscs, *Voices of the Civil Rights Movement: Black American Freedom Songs, 1960-1966* (Washington: Smithsonian Institution, Program in Black American Culture, 1980); Bernice Johnson Reagon, "Let the Church Sing 'Freedom,'" *Black Music Research Journal* 7 (1987): 105-118.

2. Thomas W. Benson, "Implicit Communication Theory in Campaign Coverage," in *Television Coverage of the 1980 Presidential Campaign*, ed. William C. Adams (Norwood, NJ: ABLEX, 1983), 104. See also Karlyn Kohrs Campbell, *Critiques of Contemporary Rhetoric* (Belmont, CA: Wadsworth, 1972); Bonnie M. Johnson, "Images of the Enemy in Intergroup Conflict," *Central States Speech Journal* 26 (1975): 84-92; E.E. White, "Solomon Stoddard's Theories of Persuasion," *Speech Monographs* 26 (1962): 235-259.

3. Henry Louis Gates, Jr., *The Signifying Monkey: A Theory of African-American Literary Criticism* (New York: Oxford University Press, 1988), xx.

4. The activists to whom I refer include a large number of people who took an active part in organizing, leading, and participating in the rhetorical acts of the civil rights movement. All of the following are

good sources of testimony of civil rights activists on the topic of singing during the movement: Carawan and Carawan, *We Shall Overcome*; Carawan and Carawan, *Freedom*; David A. DeTurk and A. Poulin, Jr., eds. *The American Folk Scene: Dimensions of the Folksong Revival* (New York: Dell, 1967); Josh Dunson, *Freedom in the Air: Song Movements of the Sixties* (New York: International, 1965); James Farmer, *Lay Bare the Heart: An Autobiography of the Civil Rights Movement* (New York: Arbor House, 1985); Henry Hampton and Steve Fayer, *Voices of Freedom: An Oral History of the Civil Rights Movement from the 1950s through the 1980s* (New York: Bantam, 1990); Julius Lester, "Freedom Songs in the South," *Broadside* 39 (Feb. 7, 1964): 1-2; Ellen Levine, ed., *Freedom's Children: Young Civil Rights Activists Tell Their Own Stories* (New York: Avon, 1993); Kay Mills, *This Little Light of Mine: The Life of Fannie Lou Hamer* (New York: Dutton, 1993); Payne, *Light of Freedom*; Howell Raines, *My Soul Is Rested: Movement Days in the Deep South Remembered* (New York: Penguin, 1977); Reagon, "In Our Hands"; Reagon, "Songs of the Civil Rights Movement"; Reagon, *Voices of the Civil Rights Movement*; Reagon, "Let the Church Sing"; Seeger and Reiser, *Everybody Says*; Robert Sherman, "Sing a Song of Freedom," in *The American Folk Scene: Dimensions of the Folksong Revival*, ed. David A. DeTurk and A. Poulin, Jr. (New York: Dell, 1967), 172-180; Elizabeth Sutherland, ed., *Letters from Mississippi* (New York: McGraw-Hill, 1965); Pat Watters, *Down To Now: Reflections on the Southern Civil Rights Movement* (New York: Random, 1971); Robert Weisbrot, *Freedom Bound: A History of America's Civil Rights Movement* (New York: W.W. Norton, 1990); Juan Williams, *Eyes on the Prize: America's Civil Rights Years, 1954-1965* (New York: Viking, 1987); Howard Zinn, *The Southern Mystique* (New York: Knopf, 1964); Howard Zinn, *SNCC: The New Abolitionists*, 2nd ed. (Boston: Beacon, 1965).

5. Gates, *Signifying Monkey*, ix.

6. Laura Crowell, "The Building of the 'Four Freedoms Speech,'" *Speech Monographs* 22 (1955): 266-283; Jill Taft-Kaufman, "Rhetorical Implications of Shakespeare's Changes in His Source Material for *Romeo and Juliet*," in *Rhetorical Dimensions in Media: A Critical Casebook*, rev. printing. Ed. Martin J. Medhurst and Thomas W. Benson (Dubuque, IA: Kendall/Hunt, 1984), 344-363.

"When the Spirit
Says Sing!"

I

Introduction

THE NEED FOR REDEFINITION OF SELF

This book advances the argument that the freedom songs of the civil rights movement were examples of purposeful communication that enabled civil rights activists to set forth a definition of themselves and their undertaking that gave impetus to movement activities. Both the act of singing and the lyrics sung contributed to a positive definition of the activists as capable of improving the conditions of African Americans in the United States.

In the middle of the 1950s, the dominant definition of blacks in America was one generated by whites and that served white interests. The perpetuators of slavery in the United States began the process, defining blacks as subhuman and writing that definition into the Constitution and the laws of the country, "declaring that each slave, for purposes of taxation and representation, would count as three-fifths of a person."[1]

During the Reconstruction period, having lost the right to own blacks outright, Southerners sought to establish other forms of domination. One of these was the perpetuation of a demeaning, and pervasive, definition of blacks. Cal Logue demonstrated that the rhetoric of southern whites was designed to define blacks around "three stock assumptions . . . that blacks were barbaric, immoral, and incapable of self-government."[2] This American "big lie" represented blacks as subhuman, and as passive and dependent on the paternalism of whites. For long years this definition was accepted by many whites and also, it seems, influenced black definitions of self.

Because of their experiences in white America, first as slaves, later as people free only in the most literal sense of no-longer-in-actual-irons,

3

blacks in America were heirs to a grim legacy. Denied decent education by Jim Crow laws, some began to believe that they could not learn. Denied decent jobs by lack of education and discrimination, some began to believe in their inability to be productive. Denied a part in the "democratic" processes, some began to believe in their impotency.

In the years leading to the civil rights movement, blacks began to acknowledge the extent to which they had adopted this white definition in spite of the limitations it placed on them. Charles Keil addressed the prevalence of self-doubt among blacks, noting that one can "pick up any document dealing with the Negro problem, and the central message whether explicit or implicit will be the same: the problem of self-hatred, the lack of self-esteem—the lack of self."[3] Keil went on to detail the changes necessary if blacks were to escape this crippling self-definition:

> more Negroes must identify themselves. They must struggle with their past and accept it—all of it; they must honor their heroes and prophets, past and present; they must define with greater care who they are now and what they want their children to become.[4]

A recognition of the potentially crippling psychological effect of the definition of blacks advanced by American society also motivated Chief Justice Warren to write, in his opinion on *Brown v. Board of Education of Topeka*, that this definition, as manifested in segregation of schools and other public facilities, created in minority children "a feeling of inferiority as to their status in the community that may affect their hearts and minds in a way unlikely ever to be undone."[5] The task that faced black Americans in the mid-twentieth century was, then, in large part, to repudiate the white definition of blacks and replace it with a definition of their own making.

The testimony of civil rights activists, as they recalled the impulse to commit their energy to the civil rights cause, suggests that they shared at least a tacit understanding of the need to replace the prevalent definition with a self-definition that would enable them to move forward. Many activists talked, in retrospect, of the self-doubts they experienced before their movement involvement. For instance, prior to her famous refusal to vacate a bus seat in Montgomery, Alabama, Rosa Parks visited Highlander Folk School. She was surprised, she recalled, when she saw, there, other African Americans able to interact comfortably with whites and plan for change. Parks's reaction was one of dismay: "I felt that I had been destroyed long ago."[6]

Melba Pattillo Beals, one of the Little Rock Nine, remembered her self-doubt, born of the ill-treatment she endured as a result of seeking admission to the all-white Central High School in Little Rock, Arkansas, in 1957:

> After a while, I started saying to myself, Am I less than human? Why did they do this to me? What's wrong with me? And so you go through the stages even as a child. First you're in pain, then you're angry, then you try to fight back, and then you just don't care. You just, you can't care; you hope you do die.[7]

Judy Tarver, an activist from Alabama, remembered of her childhood that:

> I had a white doll with blond hair. They probably didn't make a black doll. And then a lot of our people at that time were conditioned to think that maybe the lighter-skinned blacks were somehow superior to the darker. Black was not a popular word. It was a stigma if you were dark-skinned. Oh, you better not call anybody black!"[8]

Even these brave people, at the vanguard of the civil rights struggle, admitted their doubts about their worth. Bernice Johnson Reagon, one of the great songleaders of the movement, remembered the challenge of encouraging the people of her hometown to protest. She recalled that "most of the people who had lived in Albany [Georgia] all of their lives had sort of come to accept things as they were, or at least there was no outward expression of opposition to things as they were."[9] One of the tests activists faced during their tenure was to recognize the extent to which they had come to believe in the limiting definition of blacks and, perhaps, how they had been participants in it. They must also convince others, first, that it was so, and, then, that such participation must end.

Awareness of the contradictions in the prevailing definition of blacks was sparked in different ways for different people. For some African Americans, the experiences of black servicemen who had risked their lives for the United States in World War II, and who returned to segregation and oppression, was key to their reconsideration. Constance Baker Motley, an attorney for the NAACP, reflected that:

> I think people became more aware that something had to be done about the fact that black servicemen were overseas dying for this country, and when they would be coming home, they would be

coming home to a situation that said, in effect, "You're a second class citizen. You can't go to school with white children, or your children can't. You can't stay in a hotel or eat in a restaurant because you're black."[10]

Bayard Rustin, too, identified the soldiers' return as a important element in the reexamination of the place of blacks in the United States:

> I think the beginning of this period from 1954 has its roots in the returning soldiers after 1945. There was a great feeling on the part of many of these youngsters that had been away, that they had fought in the war—that they were not getting what they should have.[11]

The return of black veterans made it clear to many that African Americans were expected to live up to the responsibilities of U.S. citizenship without enjoying the incumbent rights.

For other activists, self-awareness was sparked by a growing realization of how they were seen by others. Dorothy Cotton, the Education Director for the Southern Christian Leadership Conference (SCLC), reported that:

> when a black person from another country, from Africa, visited the U.S., they said they could recognize when a person had grown up under our system, because they always walked with a little bit of a stoop, a little bit of shame.[12]

This insight helped Cotton recognize an attitude toward self held by blacks and, in recognizing it, gave her the power to address it.

Still other African Americans had crucial personal experiences that gave them insight to their flawed self-images. Ricky Shuttlesworth, daughter of movement leader Reverend Fred Shuttlesworth, went to an interracial camp at Highlander Folk School in 1960. She credited the camp experience with providing her the realization "that you are somebody and you can use your mind and develop."[13] Similarly, Fred Taylor, who participated in the Montgomery bus boycott at the age of 13, recalled experiencing a new sense of self after hearing Martin Luther King, Jr., address the subject. Taylor remembered that King

> would talk about the fact that you are somebody and you are important. This was compared to my orientation of being put down or told, "Boy, you're not going to be anything". . . . But when King

started talking, he'd say, "You are somebody." And that began to rub off on me. It was right during the [Montgomery bus] boycott that I began to have a different assessment of myself as an individual and to feel my sense of worth.[14]

Such experiences encouraged southern blacks to see the need for the redefinition of black worth and to accept the extent to which they had participated in their own oppression. They came to realize that they must, likewise, actively participate in ending this source of oppression.

Such dawning self-knowledge produced feelings of disgust and impatience in activists. Activist Marion Barry spoke of his growing awareness of the effect of the demeaning white definition:

But it makes me sick deep down inside to think that for over a hundred years the Negro has been abused, has suffered indignities bestowed upon him by the white man, has been told to go to the back, has been called inferior, and a second class citizen. I have found that I cannot continue to live with myself.[15]

Charles Sherrod communicated similar impatience and desire for change when he said that "all our lives we've had to bow and scrape, laugh when nothing was funny and scratch our heads and say 'yes sir.' We want to change that; we want to be men."[16] And Diane Nash remembered that "I couldn't believe that the children of my classmates would have to be born into a society where they had to believe that they were inferior."[17] These young people became convinced that they, and all blacks, had acted in concert with whites, and they wholeheartedly committed themselves to rejecting the definition they believed they had tacitly supported. As Dorothy Cotton put it, "Our purpose was to see how people could unbrainwash themselves."[18]

The activists' conviction that they held some responsibility for their oppression became a factor in their recruitment efforts, as they sought to persuade other young blacks to commit themselves to the movement. James Bevel urged high school students to become involved in the Birmingham campaign by arguing:

you are responsible for segregation, you and your parents, because you have not stood up. In other words, according to the Bible and the Constitution, no one has the power to oppress you if you don't cooperate. So if you say you are oppressed, then you are also acknowledging that you are in league with the oppressor; now, it's your responsibility to break league with him.[19]

The impetus for the civil rights movement came from such people, those unwilling to continue to live according to a definition relegating them to inferior status. The activists framed the situation in such a way as to accept partial responsibility for their oppression. In so doing, they suggested they were also capable of ending the oppression, by defining themselves as autonomous and repudiating the white definition of blacks.

The people who worked to kindle the flame of civil rights felt they must craft for themselves a new and positive self-definition. Only by such redefinition, a fundamental change in the way they saw themselves, could blacks effect the outward changes necessary for blacks and whites to learn to live together as equals. Such willingness to change self-definition is an important step toward doing so but the activists were also faced with finding a vehicle for such change. They argued for singing as that vehicle.

The freedom songs became an important part of the civil rights activists' attempts to construct a new sense of self. The songs offered a compelling means by which activists could communicate among themselves and disseminate a positive self-definition, and provide answers to questions about black identity and black relationships with one another and with whites. For the civil rights movement to be successful, leaders needed to encourage and motivate all blacks, not just the strong ones who had maintained self-confidence and initiative in spite of all white Americans would tell them to the contrary. All blacks in Montgomery had to be convinced to boycott the buses. Hundreds of blacks had to be motivated to march in the cities of the South. Thousands of blacks had to be urged to register to vote. For such feats to be accomplished, activists were faced with finding ways to reach these people, to overcome negative self-definitions and to redefine what in meant to be black in the South.

Activists often spoke quite pointedly about the changes they experienced during their movement participation. In general, the entire civil rights movement was defined as a new beginning for participants. E.D. Nixon, when recalling the effect Rosa Parks's arrest had on the black community, said that "the morning of December 5, 1955, the black man was reborn."[20] Of the first mass meeting in Montgomery following Parks's arrest, participant Donie Jones remembered that "it was like a revival starting. That's what it was like."[21] Sixty-year-old Topsy Eubanks attended a citizenship school, designed to prepare rural blacks to register to vote, and she, too, saw a new life beginning: "When I left, I felt like I had been born again!" Hazel T. Palmer, co-chair of the Hinds County Freedom Democratic Party, described her work as "trying to get across to people what it is to just be born."[22] Activists who took part in the movement felt that the change in themselves rivaled a rebirth.

Many of the activists targeted the songs of the movement as the key element in their revival and rebirth. When the activists spoke of the changes they experienced, they often associated those changes with the singing of freedom songs. Dorothy Cotton spoke of the re-creation she perceived as coming from the act of singing, saying, "We sang . . . songs affirming the joy of coming alive, of becoming new persons."[23] Bernice Reagon suggested that, when sung, the songs took on a power of their own. She described this power as growing beyond the control of the people who began the songs, and as a power capable of changing the very *being* of the activists. In other words, Reagon represented the freedom songs as having the power to symbolically remake the people who sang.

In her references to singing, for example, Reagon made connections between the songs and the selfhood of the singers. She claimed that, for the movement to succeed, "everyone had to sing. Everyone had to identify themselves musically."[24] Such musical identification enabled singing activists to remake themselves into people who were living refutations of the white myths regarding blacks. This argument, implicit in many of the activists' comments, was made explicit by Reagon, as she referred to changes she saw in herself, and in the people she heard sing and saw transformed.

Reagon commented on the transformation she perceived in herself, for instance, asserting that she was remade through her song:

> The voice I have now I got the first time I sang in a movement meeting, after I got out of jail. I did the song, "Over My Head I See Freedom in the Air," but I had never heard that voice before. I had never been that me before. And once I became that me, I have never let that me go.[25]

Elsewhere, she remembered the same moments, saying:

> When I opened my mouth and began to sing, there was a force and
> power within myself I had never heard before. Somehow this
> music—music I could use as an instrument to do things with, music
> that was mine to shape and change so that it made the statement I
> needed to make—released a kind of energy I did not know I had. I
> liked the feeling.[26]

Reagon described singing as an instrument or a tool she could use to
accomplish her goals, but she also argued, subtly but unequivocally,
that, by singing, she set in motion a different kind of power. The power,
according to her remarks, grew beyond her and changed her, resulting
in a new self.

Reagon asserted that the act of singing established a new sense of
self for the large groups of protestors, as well, who often responded to
outside pressure with song:

> I sat in a church and felt the chill that ran through a small gathering
> of Blacks when the sheriff and his deputies walked in. They stood at
> the door, making sure everyone knew they were there. Then a song
> began. And the song made sure that the sheriff and his deputies knew
> that we were there. We became visible, our image enlarged, when the
> sounds of the freedom songs filled all the space in that church.[27]

Here again, the songs were described as giving the singers substance
and identity where they had previously been denied—those who had
been invisible became undeniably visible when they sang. Freedom
Rider Leroi Wright, while in jail, used a similar argument to encourage
others Riders to sing with him. "Come on, let's sing some more," he
urged. "Let's let 'em know we're here and let 'em know who we
are."[28] In their talk, activists advanced the argument that, without the
rhetorical outlet of song, blacks would not have found the identity that
enabled them to go forth into the trials of the civil rights movement.

This book examines, in detail, the definition of African Americans
that emerged from the freedom songs. In placing the songs at the center
of this study, I do not intend to trivialize the work done in others areas
but, rather, to simply acknowledge the power of the songs as the
testimony of activists suggest it should be acknowledged. The songs are
the words of the masses of people who made up the marches and
demonstrations, where they tell what motivated them to risk all, where
they tell us who they would be in a changing world.

Chapter One consists of a discussion of song as a communication strategy. Activists *chose* to sing, and that choice affects the nature of the communication among activists in significant ways. Chapters Two, Three, and Four all comprise close analyses of the lyrics of the songs. In Chapter Two, I look specifically at the ways activists defined their movement goals in their songs, and at the ways they talked about themselves and set forth a self-definition. In Chapter Three, I broaden the focus to examine the ways the activists articulated their view of the world in which they struggled. It is here that I discuss the ways activists described the roles of other people, such as their adversaries and white allies, in their lives. Chapter Four is an examination of the ways activists used the songs to call for specific actions to advance the movement. In the songs, they provided themselves with information about appropriate behavior.

NOTES

1. Henry Hampton and Steve Fayer, *Voices of Freedom: An Oral History of the Civil Rights Movement from the 1950s through the 1980s* (New York: Bantam, 1990), xxv.

2. Cal Logue, "Rhetorical Ridicule of Reconstruction Blacks," *Quarterly Journal of Speech* 62 (1978): 401.

3. Charles Keil, *Urban Blues* (Chicago: University of Chicago Press, 1966), p. 165. See also Ben Sidran, *Black Talk* (New York: Holt, Rinehart and Winston, 1971), 31, 36. Sidran writes of the necessary suppression and, later, assertion of the black ego. He suggests that black music played a vital role in the reassertion of black ego.

4. Keil, *Urban Blues*, 197.

5. Ellen Levine, ed., *Freedom's Children: Young Civil Rights Activists Tell Their Own Stories* (New York: Avon, 1993), 38.

6. Rosa Parks in Pete Seeger and Bob Reiser, *Everybody Says Freedom* (New York: W.W. Norton, 1989), 25.

7. Melba Pattillo Beals in Hampton and Fayer, *Voices of Freedom*, 48-49.

8. Judy Tarver in Levine, *Freedom's Children*, 11.

9. Bernice Reagon in Hampton and Fayer, *Voices of Freedom*, 100.

10. Constance Baker Motley in Hampton and Fayer, *Voices of Freedom*, xxv.

11. Bayard Rustin in Hampton and Fayer, *Voices of Freedom*, xxvii.

12. Dorothy Cotton in Seeger and Reiser, *Everybody Says*, 15.

13. Ricky Shuttlesworth in Levine, *Freedom's Children*, 82.

14. Fred Taylor in Levine, *Freedom's Children*, 33.

15. Marion Barry in Guy Carawan and Candie Carawan, *We Shall Overcome!: Songs of the Southern Freedom Movement* (New York: Oak, 1963), 36.

16. Charles Sherrod in Carawan and Carawan, *We Shall Overcome*, 79.

17. Diane Nash in Carawan and Carawan, *We Shall Overcome*, 14.

18. Dorothy Cotton in Kay Mills, *This Little Light of Mine: The Life of Fannie Lou Hamer* (New York: Dutton, 1993), 53.

19. James Bevel in Hampton and Fayer, *Voices of Freedom*, 131-132.

20. E.D. Nixon in Seeger and Reiser, *Everybody Says*, 17.

21. Donie Jones in Hampton and Fayer, *Voices of Freedom*, 24.

22. Topsy Eubanks in Seeger and Reiser, *Everybody Says,* 121; Hazel T. Palmer in Pat Watters, *Down To Now: Reflections on the Southern Civil Rights Movement* (New York: Random, 1971), 303.

23. Dorothy Cotton in Seeger and Reiser, *Everybody Says,* 121.

24. Bernice Johnson Reagon, "Songs of the Civil Rights Movement, 1955-1965: A Study in Culture History" (Ph.D. diss., Howard University, Washington, D.C., 1975), 180.

25. Bernice Reagon in Juan Williams, *Eyes on the Prize: America's Civil Rights Years, 1954-1965* (New York: Viking, 1987), 177.

26. Bernice Johnson Reagon, "In Our Hands: Thoughts on Black Music," *Sing Out!* November 1975, 2.

27. Bernice Johnson Reagon, booklet accompanying three phonodiscs, *Voices of the Civil Rights Movement: Black American Freedom Songs, 1960-1966* (Washington: Smithsonian Institution, Program in Black American Culture, 1980), 4.

28. Leroi Wright in James Farmer, *Lay Bare the Heart: An Autobiography of the Civil Rights Movement* (New York: Arbor, 1985), 10.

II

"I Hear Singing In the Air":
Singing As Communication Strategy

> History has never known a protest movement so rich in song as the
> civil rights movement. Nor a movement in which songs are as
> important.[1]

During the years of the civil rights movement, activists sought
strategies to communicate with one another as well as with people
outside the movement's vanguard. Committed to nonviolence, the
activists searched for potentially powerful forms of communication
consistent with the ideals of the group. The people who made up the
movement were, by and large, relatively powerless as individuals, but
they chose to join together in acts designed to communicate their
unified commitment to fight injustice. They eschewed sole reliance on
traditional public address, opting often for actions that can be
considered as purposeful, or rhetorical. These actions included sit-ins,
mass demonstrations, Freedom Rides, and other forms of civil
disobedience. And during all of these gatherings, whenever the activists
met, they engaged in the behavior of singing, perhaps the most powerful
rhetorical behavior of all in the civil rights movement.

This discussion of the act of singing presumes that the activists'
choice to sing is interesting in its own right—in the United States,
singing is not that common a communication option. The activists of the
civil rights movement sang often, with clear purpose and great
confidence. The freedom songs of the civil rights were sung during
mass meetings, in jails, in churches, and in isolation, were sung by the
elderly, by college students, by children, and by those of indeterminate
age, were sung in fear, desperation, and jubilation. Activists saw these
songs, such as "We Shall Overcome," "Keep Your Eyes on the Prize,"

and "Oh Freedom" as central to their success in opposing segregation and inequality. How do we know the activists felt this way? Listen . . .

> Singing is the backbone and the balm of this movement.
>
> [Singing] is like an angel watching over you.
>
> This song represented the coming together . . . You felt uplifted and involved in a great battle and a great struggle.
>
> You sing the songs which symbolize transformation, which make that revolution of courage inside you.
>
> The movement without songs would have been like birds without wings.
>
> There was music in everything we did.
>
> One cannot describe the vitality and emotion . . . [singing] generates power that is indescribable.
>
> When you got through singing . . . you could walk over a bed of hot coals, and you wouldn't notice.
>
> There is no armor more impenetrable than song.[2]

These claims are only a few that activists have made regarding the role of the freedom songs in their lives and their struggle. They have a great deal more to tell us about their singing—how it worked for them as a strategy and why it engendered such strong feelings among them. A thorough study of their testimony about singing indicates that the activists strongly believed the songs were an essential aspect of the total persuasive strategy of the civil rights movement. Before we turn to a close study of the song lyrics, it is important to understand what the behavior of singing meant for the activists.

That the activists felt song to provide them with a special power is evident in their testimony, where they asserted that song was central to the progress of the movement. Guy Carawan was Music Director at the Highlander Folk School and in that capacity he encouraged singing among civil rights activists. Carawan made bold claims regarding the power of the songs to accomplish great things in the movement:

Freedom songs today are sung in many kinds of situations: at mass meetings, prayer vigils, demonstrations, before Freedom Rides and Sit-Ins, in paddy wagons and jails, at conferences, work-shops and informal gatherings. They are sung to bolster spirits, to gain new courage and to increase the sense of unity. The singing sometimes disarms jail guards, policemen, bystanders and mob participants of their hostilities.[3]

Bob Cohen, director of the Mississippi Caravan of Music, similarly addressed the far-reaching effects of the singing when he argued that "somehow you can go in the face of violence and death, cynicism and inaction of the FBI, the indifference of the Federal Government when you can sing with your band of brothers."[4] According to these activists, singing provided movement participants with significant power to face the internal enemies of fear and doubt as well as the external trials of the movement.

When the activists spoke of their singing and its effects, it was often in tones of awe, as if they could not quite believe what their singing could accomplish. In speaking of the unofficial anthem of the movement, "We Shall Overcome," Wyatt Tee Walker said simply that "it generates power that is indescribable."[5] Candie Carawan recounted her experience in jail and her realization there that songs could be more than a source of entertainment. She said, "Never had I heard such singing. Spirituals, pop tunes, hymns, and even slurpy old love songs all became so powerful."[6] Even onlookers to the movement, such as white journalist Pat Watters, were affected by the mood of the mass meetings—"mystical, inspired and excited, ecstatic"—and the music there that "cannot be described—or recaptured."[7] These people, and seemingly all others who experienced the singing of the civil rights movement, cast song as a motive force in that struggle, a force giving the participants the strength to move forward and to involve others.

The songs figured so greatly in the minds of some activists that they expressed doubt that the movement could progress or succeed without singing. Bernice Reagon, for instance, claimed that "by the end of the Freedom Rides, the songs of the Sit-ins, bus and jail experiences were considered essential for organizing. No mass meeting could be successfully carried off without songs."[8] Both Cordell Reagon and Student Nonviolent Coordinating Committee (SNCC) field secretary Charles Jones remarked on the centrality of the songs to the campaign in Albany, Georgia. According to Reagon,

without the songs, the Albany movement could not have been. They
sang these songs on the [picket] line and off the line, day in and day
out, and went to bed humming "We Shall Overcome."

Jones's words echoed Reagon's when he said simply "there could have
been no Albany Movement without music."[9] In singing, activists felt
they had found an activity that united them, shielded them from harm,
and gave them the very power and strength to move forward.

It might be argued, of course, that the activists had no evidence of
any link between singing and the powers they attributed to it. The
important consideration is not whether singing actually allowed activists
to accomplish all the things they claimed for it but, rather, that they
believed it did. If activists believed singing provided them with the
strength to face difficult situations, then, when they sang, they were
likely to find that, in fact, they did feel stronger. The claims they made
about the communicative power of song fostered an attitude toward
singing among participants in the movement, and gave this form of
communication enormous power in their lives—the power that comes
with expectations.

Scholars suggest that singing differs from other forms of
communication, in that it more fully involves those who take part.
Rhetorical critics argue that musical sound engages human feeling in
significant ways because its kinesthetic appeal promotes a physiological
and psychological response.[10] In many forms of demonstration, civil
rights activists were involved both by their physical presence and by the
act of protest—whether it was marching, sitting-in, or swaying with the
music of a song. In addition, when the activists sang, their involvement
grew to include not only their presence and physical movement, all
rhetorical insofar as they constituted purposeful action, but the voicing
of their commitment as well.

Singing was most often engaged in during other types of
demonstration, which added another layer of communication to the mass
marches. The communication of the movement was usually much more
than a single voice speaking in a quiet room to silent listeners. Instead,
it was a rich mixture of singing, listening, marching, swaying, and other
symbolic acts. The involvement was much greater and, potentially,
much more influential when communication had several layers of
expression.

Singing was, perhaps, most important to activists when other
symbolic acts were denied them. According to the activists, some of the

most fervent and inspired singing in the movement took place in the cells of Parchman Penitentiary and the Hinds County Jail in Mississippi where the Freedom Riders were imprisoned. In jail, many other forms of direct action were denied the activists but, in singing, they were able to find a positive rhetorical place between passivity and acts of violence. Euvester Simpson referred to time she spent in jail as a result of trying to register to vote, and remarked that the "only way we could get through that ordeal was to sing any song that came to mind."[11] By singing, the activists continued to communicate their refusal to be rendered impotent or to be drawn to the level of their adversaries. Their jailers recognized the power that their prisoners held when they sang and often threatened the activists. Zinn reported that:

> Charles Sherrod had been taken with a group of demonstrators to "Terrible" Terrell County, escorted there by Sheriff Zeke Mathews, who announced: "There'll be no damn singin' and no damn prayin' in *my* jail."[12]

For civil rights activists, the choice of music as a mode of communication was a choice consistent with their desire to act and their belief that song was essentially symbolic act. It complemented the other acts of the civil rights movement and sometimes stood alone, or combined with prayer, as the only positive communication outlet available to the protestors.

The activists' belief in the power of song and its "correctness" for meeting their needs meant that activists often chose singing even when other options, like speaking, were available. In their comments, activists equated song with speech or, often, asserted that song did for them what speech could not. Bob Cohen's description of Fannie Lou Hamer indicated that, for this particular black leader, song was used in essentially the same way that speeches were:

> When Mrs. Hamer finishes singing a few freedom songs one is aware that he has truly heard a fine political speech, stripped of the usual rhetoric and filled with the anger and determination of the civil rights movement. And on the other hand in her speeches there is the constant thunder and drive of music.[13]

Cohen's comments equated political speaking and singing but he also subtly argued for the superiority of singing when he claimed that song retained its power without the bombast and meaningless words so often associated with political speaking.

Speech was insufficient not only for black leaders like Hamer but for the average person as well, according to the activists. Bernice Reagon claimed that, in Albany, Georgia, "masses of people had much to say about their condition and found the language with which to speak in the songs."[14] Whether the implication here was that these people were inarticulate in their speaking or that they were not listened to when they spoke is less important than the assertion that they found an outlet to overcome such difficulties.

Activists also described themselves as turning to song when they were so overwhelmed by one emotion or another that speaking seemed not to fulfill their desire to communicate. One described a preacher as follows:

> The sermon began as a talk and ended as a song. The preacher jumped up and down and had tears running down his face. He finally was overcome by the sheer power of his words and started singing "This Little Light of Mine" in the middle of a sentence.[15]

Josh Dunson, in his book *Freedom in the Air,* also commented on the tendency for song to take over when speech fell short, saying, "often, emotion is too strong to come out in words, so a new song is born."[16] The activists promoted their songs as providing a special outlet for their excitement and fears, an outlet unavailable elsewhere.

As an outlet for strong emotion, song became, according to the activists, more forceful and vital than speech. Although logic dictates that southern police would have as much power to silence singing activists as chanting or speaking activists, movement participants felt the singing was less likely to be quelled. Bernice Reagon argued that "with a song, there was nothing they could do to block what we were saying," while Willie Peacock also commented that, when activists sang, "there is nothing the police can do to stop you. They can put you in jail, but you can sing in jail."[17] Reagon seems to have summed up the attitude of the activists when she said, simply, that, for blacks in the civil rights movement, "the songs were more powerful than spoken conversation."[18]

The commentary of the songleaders indicates that they emphatically did not conceive of the singing that accompanied nearly every aspect of the movement as merely expressive or as entertainment. Although these are often accepted as the functions of song, the singers in the civil rights movement held the strong belief that song communicated and, in fact, did so in ways that surpassed speech.

It is worthwhile to know that the activists held strong faith in their singing but questions remain regarding the source of the power of song. What about singing made that particular behavior stand out as powerful in the activists' minds? It is clear that the special appeal of singing came, in part, from the long tradition of protest singing in African-American culture.

THE AFRICAN AMERICAN SONG TRADITION

The songs sung during the civil rights movement were drawn, primarily, from black tradition. Some had their roots in the songs of slavery and in the years immediately following the Civil War. Others appeared later in African American tradition, as gospel songs. Still others came to the tradition from black laborers who took part in the labor movements of the 1930s and 1940s, where protest singing was considered an important aspect of the struggle. The existence of such a longstanding tradition created a special context for singing in the civil rights movement.

The tradition of singing among Africans and African Americans is a long and tenacious one. When the first Africans were brought to America in large numbers as slaves, they brought with them a musical tradition that has remained important in black life, and that differs from many Western conceptions of music.[19] Black music scholars argue that in many African cultures, music has traditionally been a pervasive element in daily life. John Lovell wrote of the African tradition of the "integrating of every action and thought into song, and of song into every thought and action,"[20] and Gerhard Putschogl concurred, saying that, "it cannot be stressed enough that black music and 'black life' cannot be separated. Both influence and depend on each other."[21] Scholars also note the extent to which all people, not just designated "entertainers," made singing one of their primary forms of communication in African cultures. As Lovell put it, the "African rarely plays *for* someone as Westerners do; he usually plays *with* someone. An inactive audience to a musical performance simply does not exist."[22]

Singing and music, then, were common and acknowledged forms of communication for many African people.

One of the many roles singing played in African life was in the maintaining of positive relationships with others. Some Africans believed it was important for a person to express strong feelings in order to be healthy, but they also considered it inappropriate to *speak* these feelings.[23] It was understood, though, that "you can say publicly in songs what you cannot say privately to a man's face."[24] The use of song, as well as the development of masking devices, such as circumlocution and double entendre, allowed Africans to express strong feelings in subtle ways, unlikely to invite repercussions.

Singing as a form of social commentary was a tradition that might have faded when black slaves were exposed to white culture, but instead it grew stronger. The skills of singing and the use of subtle and purposely ambiguous language remained strong in African American life simply because the situation faced by African slaves in America reinforced the need for such techniques. Slave owners and overseers used certain tactics, in hopes of ensuring the docility of their slaves, and created an atmosphere in which singing flourished.

The most obvious means by which slave owners sought to oppress slaves was in their attempts to limit interaction among slaves. Owners were aided in this endeavor by the fact that slaves had been brought to America from all over Africa, and often shared little or nothing in the way of culture with the other Africans with whom they lived and worked. As Sydney Mintz and Richard Price asserted:

> these were not *communities* of people at first, and they could only become communities by processes of cultural exchange. What the slaves undeniably shared at the outset was their enslavement; all—or nearly all—else had to be *created by them*.[25]

Whites then sought to reinforce this distance among slaves by restricting talk and meetings among slaves. They did, however, encourage the singing of songs, which, to them, seemed evidence that their slaves were content and productive.

The slaves used both the act of singing and the words of the songs to overcome their cultural differences and to bypass white restrictions on their interaction. By doing so, they succeeded in building community and in uniting themselves with others in their group. From this position of unification, they were better equipped to resist white oppression.

The nature of white oppression of African and African American slaves was built on the premise that, for people to be fully conquered, they must come to doubt themselves and their own worth. While individuals can be coerced to behave in any number of ways, I. Ira Goldenberg has argued that "people only become oppressed when they have been forced (either subtly or with obvious malice) to finally succumb to the insidious process that continually undermines hope and subverts the desire to 'become.'" This self-doubt and belief in one's inferiority is the hallmark of oppression.[26]

In white Americans' attempts to oppress black slaves in the United States, the creation of self-doubt played an important role. White owners and overseers advanced limiting definitions of the slaves and sought to convince them that they were fit only for slavery. The black slave was defined by whites, variously, as three-fifths a human being, as chattel, and as a barbaric heathen.[27]

The clear message slaves received from their masters concerned their inferiority. Kenneth Stampp reported that whites strove "to implant in the bondsmen themselves a consciousness of personal inferiority . . . They had to feel that African ancestry had tainted them, that their color was a badge of degradation."[28] Shortly after the Nat Turner rebellion in 1831, a delegate to the Virginia legislature articulated this goal of southern whites:

> We have as far as possible closed every avenue by which light may enter slaves' minds. If we could extinguish the capacity to see the light our work would be completed; they would then be on a level with the beasts of the field.[29]

In numerous ways, white owners contrived to constrain black life by controlling the definitions applied to slaves.

Slaves drew on their prior experience as singers and on their skill at hiding meaning in language to provide themselves with a potent communication outlet. When white slave owners and overseers sought to advance limiting definitions of the slaves, to convince them that they were fit only for slavery, singing became for slaves a means by which to resist such definitions, as it would, one hundred years or more later, for civil rights activists. The slave spirituals have been widely recognized as a primary means by which slaves resisted oppression and an indication to all who hear them of the slaves "determination to *be* in a society that [sought] to eliminate their being."[30]

From these early roots there evolved many types of black music, secular and sacred, that continued to function to provide African Americans with ways to define themselves and to communicate about social action. The conditions faced by blacks in America have continued to reinforce the singing tradition and to make singing an important rhetorical outlet for blacks. Thomas F. Jones, in his thesis on black song from 1860 until 1930, indicated that after the Civil War blacks continued to rely on their musical heritage. Although Emancipation and the war had ended legalized slavery, African Americans were still at an unbearable disadvantage in white America. During this time,

> the songs of the black church maintained many of the uses of the earlier spirituals in expressing ideas of encouragement and comfort found in the Christian religion and in adapting those ideas to the particular needs of a people suffering social oppression.[31]

Jones discussed themes of sacred music and of the evolving black secular music, the blues, and suggested that the songs continued to be used rhetorically to establish a sense of identity. In the Reconstruction period, "singing among blacks provided both a means of individual self-expression and a collective sense of identity and community."[32] According to Jones's findings, free blacks in America found music and singing to be of continuing importance in their lives.

More recently, according to scholars in the field of African American music, jazz and the blues have become important links in the chain African Americans have wrought with their song. Charles Keil cited the clarifying and integrating of a positive sense of being as a key function of singing the blues. Labeling black entertainers "identity experts," Keil credited them, at all stages of African experience in America, with acting as invaluable spokespeople for their brethren. Sidran argued similarly that jazz became the "urban voice of the black culture."[33]

Because black music has served so extensively as a means of establishing identity it is apparent that all black music in America is, essentially, protest music. Black music has enabled its creators and performers to resist attempts to define African Americans in negative and limiting ways. Sidran claimed that "through the years, music has been the major survival tactic for black America."[34] The survival to which Sidran referred is the survival of black culture and of a sense of black worth.

When the activists for civil rights searched for strategies in their continuation of the black struggle for freedom and equality, they came to recognize the rhetorical potential of the traditional songs of black culture. Strong and enduring, free of many of the constraints limiting other communication options, the singing tradition of their ancestors provided activists with an outlet for feelings and assertions. The activists did not, however, adopt these older songs without some ambivalence.

THE SELF AS BLACK

During the late nineteenth and early twentieth centuries, while some forms of black music flourished, many blacks had come to see the old, religious songs and the traditional way of singing them as something of which African Americans should be embarrassed. Many blacks distanced themselves from what they saw as an overly emotional style of singing and from songs that were associated with slavery. Lawrence Levine related the story of Robert Russa Moton, the man who succeeded Booker T. Washington as head of Tuskegee Institute, who remembered hearing the singing of spirituals when he entered Hampton Normal and Agricultural Institute at the age of 18, in 1885:

> Though Moton had known these songs all of his life, they were so beautifully performed that he was deeply moved. He was also deeply disappointed to hear plantation songs sung by educated people in an educational institution: "I had come to school to learn to do things differently; to sing, to speak, and to use the language, and of course, the music, not of coloured people, but of white people."

When other students argued that the spirituals were worthy of singing Moton remembered that the "only reply I could give was that they were Negro songs and that we had come to Hampton to learn something better"[35] James P. Blake, a teacher in the Georgia Sea Islands, also believed that students should be discouraged from singing black songs, and wrote about their anxiety in singing them, saying, "I have seen them, when requested to sing some of their grotesque hymns, which were great favorites in slave-times, hide their heads while singing, and seem heartily ashamed of them."[36] Such teachings were bound to create a residual ambivalence among blacks.

Perhaps it is not surprising, then, that even though civil rights activists remember singing at the earliest mass meetings, it took some time and much debate before they adopted songs from the black tradition. The inclusion of singing at the early meetings resulted, in part, from the fact that those meetings were held in churches, and congregational singing played an important role in other church-oriented gatherings. The songs sung at that stage were consistent with the church setting and indicated the distance African Americans had traveled away from their traditional roots. Many of the songs were those learned from church hymnals. Coretta Scott King remembered that the people who gathered for meetings during the Montgomery bus boycott sang hymns such as "What a Friend We Have in Jesus," "What a Fellowship, What a Joy Divine, Leaning on the Everlasting Arm," and "Lord, I Want to Be a Christian in My Heart."[37] Likewise, Julius Lester recalled that "they sang the Battle Hymn of the Republic to death."[38] Guy Carawan, of Highlander Folk School in Tennessee, began to teach songs to representatives of black communities gathered at Highlander and at other planning sessions, and found that the "more educated Negroes had lost their tradition of spiritual singing and were using songs like 'Onward Christian Soldiers' . . . to rally spirits."[39] The impulse toward singing was apparent in these early days of the movement but song was yet to become a well-planned strategy for the activists.

As the movement gathered momentum and activists began to think more strategically, Carawan, among others, recognized "the potential for a great singing movement in the Negro struggle."[40] For this to occur, activists needed to find a body of songs appropriate to the goals of the movement. As Reverend C.T. Vivian noted, many of the songs that came to activists' minds failed to address civil rights concerns:

> When we did start seeking songs to use at mass meetings, the only thing we had among us that had any sense of life to it was church music. And some of the church music didn't fit at all. For instance, I was giving a movement speech once, and the choir followed with 'I'll Fly Away' . . . it was a direct contradiction to what I was saying.[41]

The search for suitable material took activists to their cultural roots.

In the place of white hymns and songs like "The Battle Hymn of the Republic," Carawan reintroduced traditional black songs, like "We Shall Overcome," "Keep Your Eyes on the Prize," and "We Shall Not

Be Moved." Many activists embraced these traditional songs, but some others associated the old songs with the days of black enslavement, and argued the songs should be forgotten as remnants of a demeaning time. The arguments for the adoption of the songs from the black tradition proved to be compelling, and bear reviewing because they provide insight to the strategy planning in which the activists engaged. The reasons given for embracing the old songs also indicate the self-definition toward which activists moved.

As activists discussed the appropriateness of the old songs, many cast the singing of traditional songs as a vital return to their past and a recognition of their heritage, a heritage of which they felt they must learn to be proud. Carawan observed, for example, that:

> for some Negro college students, as well as for some adults, this revival of spiritual singing has meant a turning back to a part of their cultural heritage—an embracing of something which for years they have scorned or rejected.[42]

When activists talked about the singing of these songs, they redefined their ideas of what it meant to be black—to choose the old songs was to recognize their own heritage and to express pride in it.

In one of many debates on the value of singing the old songs, Len Chandler discussed his coming to terms with his heritage and his new appreciation for traditional black music:

> I went through this scene, man. I was ashamed of my Grandmother's music. I went to school to get the degree, in Akron, and things were all put up in a nice little box, a package of the Western World's music. But there was nothing in that box about my music. Why even the spirituals were fitted out for a white audience, made to sound nice and polite. . . . It wasn't until this white professor took me to his house to listen to some tapes that I started to know what my music is about. It took a white man to teach me—about my own music! Why this music . . . is great.[43]

Chandler's remarks convey a certain amazement and surprise—a young man, realizing for the first time, it seems, that a valuable part of his cultural heritage had been lost to him. Others were reaching the same realization, and argued that the return to traditional black culture, eschewing the cultural preferences of the white culture surrounding them, was a step toward establishing a sense of self-worth among black people. Carawan wrote of the impact of the old music on young people who had been "brainwashed by the public school system to accept the myth of their own inferiority." He recalled that the discovery of the rich tradition of black music came to these young activists as an "exhilarating revelation."[44]

Part of the realization to which activists were coming was that black music had beauty and eloquence and that it belonged to them in ways white music never could. They found strength in singing the songs that defined them as people from a certain heritage and a certain past. The songs, they asserted as they discussed singing and refined its use as a rhetorical strategy, were an especially appropriate tool for advancing the black cause, because they had been used effectively so often in the past.

The attitude that developed among activists was one of ownership—the songs were theirs. Bernice Reagon repeatedly referred back to the exact moment, at a movement meeting after a stint in jail, when she first "had the awareness that these [traditional] songs were mine and I could use them for what I needed."[45] Bessie Jones, too, argued that the old music should be adopted simply because "it is our own. It came from ourselves."[46] Andrew Young, then of the Southern Christian Leadership Conference, endorsed the singing of the songs of black tradition and generalized that "we all know that you can't trust a Negro on a negotiating committee who doesn't like his people's music."[47] Activists acknowledged the place of black culture in their movement to better black lives.

Once they began to claim ownership of the songs, activists actively developed a traditional song repertoire. In so doing, they were quick to reclaim songs as their own, even when those songs had been shunned or forgotten for years. The most notable instance of such reclamation was "We Shall Overcome." The song that has become so completely associated with the civil rights movement was originally a black hymn but it had fallen from the repertoires of African American singers. It had been preserved at Highlander Folk School, where the directors had taught it to protestors in the labor union movement in the 1940s, and it was from Guy Carawan that civil rights activists learned the song. Reagon's definition of this process stressed the feeling among activists that the song never stopped belonging to blacks:

Highlander had served only as custodian of the song. They had kept
it alive by using it as a song of struggle but were proud to be able to
see it reclaimed by Black people. And reclaimed it was.[48]

So completely did blacks feel ownership for this song in particular
that many had distinctly negative reactions to Lyndon Johnson's use of
the words "we shall overcome" in his speech asking Congress for a
voting rights bill in 1965. In that address, Johnson asserted that "it is
not just Negroes but all of us who must overcome the crippling legacy
of bigotry and injustice. And we shall overcome."[49] Far from
establishing common ground with blacks, Johnson caused many to
dissociate themselves from the song when he borrowed it for his
purposes. Juan Williams wrote of the way Johnson's use of the words
raised questions among activists, and Reagon argued that "President
Lyndon B. Johnson's use of 'We Shall Overcome' ended the
effectiveness of that song as the theme song of the Civil Rights
Movement."[50] Johnson, the leader of white America, co-opted the
words, incorporating them within the established order and, in the
activists' minds, undercutting their value as a statement indicating
movement away from that established order.[51]

Beyond its appeal as a symbol of black culture, many activists cast
singing as a particularly effective communication tool that would serve
civil rights activists as it had served earlier generations. Cordell Reagon
suggested that singing had provided the impetus enabling generations of
blacks to change their lives. He argued that "without these songs, you
know we wouldn't be anywhere. We'd still be down on Mister
Charley's plantation, chopping cotton for 30 cents a day."[52]

The activists felt confident that singing would work for their needs
because it had been tested repeatedly by their ancestors. They spoke of
the old songs as a legacy from their ancestors that had "remained in the
Black community after the days of slavery were over, to be adapted and
changed again and again in times of crisis."[53] Reagon argued that the
slavery songs and the civil rights songs both focused on relationships
between blacks and whites and, for this reason, "the slave and Civil
War songs could be used with only minor word changes needed to
update the traditional situation."[54] Carawan, too, highlighted the
perceived similarities between the two situations in observing that "no
other songs have been able to express so closely the feelings of the
participants or have been so easily adapted to the current situations as
some of the old spirituals."[55] By singing the songs of earlier black

resistance, activists symbolically linked themselves to those who had fought earlier. They implicitly defined themselves in certain ways, focusing not only on the people of the past but on the symbolic choices their ancestors made in seeking to improve their lives.

In these ways, activists recognized that the singing of traditional songs was a tested and proven strategy used by generations of southern blacks to better their lives. The degree to which blacks made music a part of their quest for an improved sense of personal and group worth has led to one of the most pervasive stereotypes white Americans hold regarding African Americans—the belief that blacks have an inherent affinity and talent for music. Julius Lester addressed this confusion in his observation that "the Negro became stereotyped as a people who loved to sing when it would have been more accurate to say that they were a people who had to sing."[56] Singing among African Americans evolved into a cultural strength because song, first, was *necessary* and, second, was reinforced in the churches and in other fora for black expression. Because of the role music had played, and continues to play, in black life, most participants in the civil rights movement had a great deal of prior experience as creators and singers of songs. The movement benefitted from a large core of people who could and did sing well, not because it was in their genes, but because their heritage of dealing with oppression had prepared them in a certain way. Of all the means of persuasion available to activists, music was most comfortable to many southern blacks and the one at which they could appear their strongest and most able.[57]

From the foregoing comments, it is evident that the activists argued for the possibility and value of learning communication strategies from others in similar situations. They recognized that their ancestors had wrought significant changes in their lives with song—other African Americans before them had articulated their right to exist and had resisted the limiting definitions put forth by whites. The activists held that singing would enable them to advance their cause in similar ways.

Underlying all of the talking about the value of singing the traditional songs was a strong sense of identification with the people who had come before them. Singing served as a reminder that the civil rights struggles were part of something larger—that the hardships were a microcosm for the struggles of all blacks in America. On any given day, activists might engage in the specific act of sitting in at a lunch counter, but their singing reminded them of the larger context for the specific acts. The activists endured the humiliation of stoically sitting while whites covered them with catsup and sugar from the lunch counters. They sat through these smaller humiliations because they kept their "eyes on the prize" of larger goals towards which blacks had been working for generations, while enduring untold suffering on the way. The songs served as important reminders of the past and the heritage from which the African Americans of the 1960s came, identifying them in spirit with brave ancestors who had voiced words of protest in years past.

Activists seemed eager to be reminded, partly through the act of singing, of the history of black oppression. Such reminders no doubt fueled their resolve. They seemed, especially, to look for inspiration to the years blacks had spent in servitude. Singer Bessie Jones, in urging the adoption of the traditional songs, chose to remind doubters of the role singing had played in black history:

> The only place where we could say we did not like slavery, say it for ourselves to hear, was in these old songs. We could not read and the master thought he could trap us with no existence and we could do nothing about it. But we did . . . with the music.[58]

As fully as Jones wanted the past to be recognized, some younger activists also sought reminders of the trials their ancestors had faced. Amanda Bowens, for instance, defended the singing of the old songs because she seemed to feel they might provide her with special insight:

> I want to know what the old songs are. I want to sing them. I want to know that my parents were working for 15 cents a day. What these songs are is what most of this means.[59]

Martin Luther King, Jr., remarked similarly that "one could not help but be moved by these traditional songs, which brought to mind the long history of the Negro's suffering."[60] Such reminders of the scope of oppression faced by blacks may have served to sustain Bowens and others like her when they faced the difficulties of movement life.

In many ways, the choice to sing the traditional songs from black history lent a sense of continuity to the contemporary struggle, linking it, in the minds of the activists, to the ongoing struggles of African Americans in the United States. Activists cast themselves as reliving the struggles of their ancestors. They identified closely with the ways black slaves and other generations of blacks had resisted oppression through one of the few communication outlets available to them—song. The activists stressed these links and argued that they could benefit from drawing on the strategies of the past.

The activists chose to incorporate these old songs into their repertoire instead of the kinds of music currently popular among young people. Although activists sometimes sang new songs and parodies of popular songs, the songs from black tradition, the freedom songs, were deemed more universally appropriate and appealing. Bernice Reagon notes that the old songs lent themselves particularly well to the needs of activists, because they addressed the same issues of relationships between blacks and whites important to civil rights protestors. Songs based on rhythm and blues were sung informally, to ease tensions, but "freedom songs with a religious basis were sung in any arena: in jails, in meetings, rallies, and on marches."[61] Such comments suggest that the protestors believed the old songs enabled them to communicate differently than did any other form of communication available to them.

A precedent set by their black ancestors convinced activists that singing was a useful and effective rhetorical choice. Civil rights workers drew on the traditions of their heritage as blacks in America to build a communication strategy in which singing played a key role. They made a conscious choice to include singing as an integral part of their movement because they saw singing, and the old songs, as particularly appropriate for their rhetorical needs. In doing so, they implicitly set about redefining how they saw themselves—they chose to celebrate being black.

EMOTIONALISM AND SPIRITUALITY

Just as activists had to reacquaint themselves with the songs of black tradition, they found that the singing style traditionally associated with African American music was alien to many of them as well. This style was highly emotional and passionate, with singers often transcending inhibitions and releasing intense feelings.

When many African Americans had learned that they should feel ashamed of the old songs of their heritage so, too, had they been urged away from a singing style deemed unseemly and inappropriate. Mahalia Jackson remembered that, as a music student, her teachers urged her to change her style. One teacher stopped Jackson in the middle of singing "Standing in the Need of Prayer," to say to tell her to "stop hollering." "The way you sing," the teacher argued, "is not a credit to the Negro race. You've got to learn to sing songs so that white people can understand them."[62] Fannie Lou Hamer recognized the extent to which blacks had been dissuaded from singing in the emotional style of their tradition, especially when she visited Africa. Biographer Mills noted that Hamer saw that "Africans had a sense of physical freedom in their artistic performances that Mrs. Hamer felt black Americans, particularly black Mississippians, had been forced to repress. After her evenings watching the African performers, she comments: 'It's not unclean, it's just innocent people, you know, just pure innocence. . . . And that was really beautiful to me.'"[63] Carawan also wrote of "those educated type of Negroes who have gotten rid of all traces of folk speech, humor, and old Baptist style in their behavior and are afraid to sing a spiritual or gospel song that might cause a foot to tap, hands to clap or bodies to sway."[64] He, too, encouraged singers to rediscover this style. Many activists in the civil rights movement did, indeed, reclaim the emotional style of singing, just as they had reclaimed the traditional songs.

In their comments about the place of singing in the movement, activists frequently mentioned the spirit and feeling engendered by singing. They stressed the emotional involvement of the singers and the ways song increased emotional commitment to the movement. The songs, they suggested, encouraged singers to exhibit a degree of emotionalism and spirituality that had been lost as black intellectuals had rejected their past. The talk about the emotional release and its value for the civil rights movement no doubt created a reassuring context in which activists could take the risks involved in setting aside their inhibitions.

The highly emotional style was featured by activists, in their testimony, as both appealing and necessary to movement progress. Carawan stressed the emotion of the singing when he remarked that when the old songs were "sung with anything approximating the old time spirit and style, they are unbeatable."[65] Reagon described the intensity of the emotion and participation characteristic of the mass meetings where everyone sang:

> There was a woman at the Shiloh Baptist Church who would sing one song, "Come and Go With Me to That Land," for an hour. It was not a song anymore. People are clapping, the feet are going and you

could hear her three blocks away. Your ears are not enough, your
eyes are not enough, your body is not enough, and you can't block it.
The only way you can survive the singing is to open up and let go
and be moved by it to another space.[66]

SNCC field secretary Charles Sherrod also described the force of
emotion at the meetings, in terms somewhat similar to Reagon's:

The church was packed before eight o'clock. People were
everywhere. . . . When the last speaker among the students, Bertha
Gober, had finished, there was nothing left to say. Tears filled the
eyes of hard, grown men who had seen with their own eyes merciless
atrocities committed. . . . And when we rose to sing "We Shall
Overcome," nobody could imagine what kept the church on four
corners. . . . I threw my head back and sang with my whole body.[67]

Reagon and Sherrod both described the emotion as something that grew
and seemed to become too large for the space containing it, building in
its power to change and move people in profound ways.

Elsewhere, Reagon remembered the mass singing in a similar way,
suggesting it generated emotion capable of elevating people to a new
level. She said:

I saw people in church sing and pray until they shouted. I knew *that*
music as a part of a cultural expression that was powerful enough to
take people from their conscious selves to a place where the physical
and intellectual being worked in harmony with the spirit.[68]

Reagon also described the "mini-revolution" that took place inside of
people when they sang in the movement:

It is like stepping off into space . . . Your body gets flushed, you
tremble, you're tempted to turn off the circuits. But that's when you
have to turn up the burner and commit yourself to follow that song
wherever it leads.[69]

Their singing was an outlet that activists suggested allowed them to
communicate their intense feelings and dedication.

Similar references to unbridled feeling responses in the singing of
the movement abound, with activists commenting on the feeling and
emotion that filled them and moved them to a new level of

commitment. Songs were seen both as a way to create emotion in people and as a way to release emotion. Negative emotions gave way to positive in Cordell Reagon's account of times when painful discussions or tensions arose among activists as they did their work:

> Anybody, not a singer or anything, just anybody at the meeting or in the office, would open up with a line of a song, and somebody else would take it over, and somebody else would add a verse, and by the end, everybody would be hugging each other and loving each other. You can't have a movement without that.[70]

The songs were said to evoke "vitality and emotion," and to be the outlet for "suppressed hope, suffering, even joy and love" as well as for "sadness and gladness of heart."[71]

In their talk, activists constructed an argument that represented emotionalism as a key part of the appeal of the singing, something that went far beyond intellectual commitment to the cause. The number and nature of the comments made regarding an emotional involvement generated by singing suggests that the activists placed great value on that characteristic. They argued for total involvement, and found a communication strength in a traditional communication style. According to Cordell Reagon, the emotional involvement inherent in the freedom singing gave activists an edge over others:

> Everybody—they put themselves into it [the singing]. . . . Most people would be ashamed to involve themselves in something like this, because they think it's kind of barbaric. . . . But down here it is a very common thing. They don't feel ashamed that they are letting the inner part of them out. . . . They have an advantage over most Americans.[72]

The emotionalism was important, according to the activists, not only because it was involving but it implied a risk-taking, an opening of the self, and a trust in others that activists felt were necessary for the movement to succeed. They were engaged in redefining, for themselves, what was shameful and what was admirable.

Related to this emphasis on a return to a more emotional style, the activists asserted that the revival of the old songs also transformed the people in the movement by returning them to a more spiritual foundation. Hollis Watkins suggested this as a strategy for reaching the people of the South, saying, "If you are black and from the South, especially Mississippi, there is a special element that is part of you. When you organize here, you are working and organizing among religious people."[73] The traditional songs, almost always bearing some religious or spiritual references, became a way to tap into the preexisting spirituality of the people the activists sought to reach.

The activists associated their singing, according to their comments about it, with a spirituality that constituted their essence and motivated them. Many of their comments referred to the songs as expressions from the "spirit" or the "souls" of the singers,[74] as the "spirit" of the movement,[75] or as a means by which singers could raise their "spirits."[76] Fannie Lou Hamer, one of the most acclaimed of the civil rights song leaders, commented on the singing, saying that it "is very important. It brings out your soul."[77]

James Farmer remembered Jim Bevel's use of a metaphor that associated singing with the souls of the activists. While the Freedom Riders were in Parchman Penitentiary, they sang freedom songs. The guards ordered them to stop singing, and threatened to take away the only bit of comfort they had—their mattresses. Farmer recalled:

> People were quiet for a while, until finally Jim Bevel, who was a Bible student at the time, made a little speech pointing out, "What they're trying to do is take your soul away. It's not the mattress, it's your soul." Then everybody said, "Yes, yes, we'll keep our soul." One Freedom Rider then yelled, "Guards, guards, guards," and the guards came dashing out to the cellblock to see what was wrong. He said, "Come get my mattress. I'll keep my soul."[78]

The activists represented their singing as a manifestation of their souls and stressed the spirituality they believed was inherent in the singing.

Activists associated singing and spirituality in other instances as well. Esau Jenkins, a singer from Johns Island, S.C., referred to the old songs as the expression of "people who sang from oppressed soul and need."[79] Reagon described the effect of the opening songs on a mass meeting, suggesting that after the songs were finished, "there was a feeling that the meeting had officially begun and had developed its own spiritual power and pace."[80] Some activists described the group unity that they claimed was created by singing in terms elevating it beyond the unity established by a common goal and stressing spirituality. Willie Peacock explained it, saying:

> When you sing, you can reach deep into yourself and communicate
> some of what you've got to other people, and you get them to reach
> inside of themselves. You release your soul force, and they release
> theirs, until you can feel like you are part of one great soul.[81]

The effect of such an intense joining provided activists, according to
Cordell Reagon, with a "something unbelievable, a total spiritual
experience." The singing, according to Reagon, also provided a
protection for activists that he likened to a spiritual protection. In his
words, the "music kept us together and kept us less afraid. It's like an
angel watching over you."[82]

Other testimony reinforces the importance of themes of religion and
spirituality for activists, and associates this spirituality with the act of
singing. One of the most revered songleaders in the movement was
Fannie Lou Hamer, who was described as "praying that prayer which
the song carries," while the secretary of the Albany campaign, Goldie
Jackson, recalled the first meeting of that campaign in terms that closely
associated singing and praying:

> I'll never forget it. It was on a Sunday night at the Mount Zion
> Baptist Church. . . . That night we sang "We Shall Overcome" for the
> first time. We are a very emotional people anyway. Two things we
> knew held us together: prayer of something good to come and song
> that tells from the depth of the heart how we feel about our fellow
> man. People stayed there all night long that first time, praying and
> singing.[83]

In many of their comments, activists spoke of "singing and praying" as
if the two acts were irrevocably bound together, combining the two
repeatedly in their comments. Jackson, for instance, remembered the
first night of that campaign, saying, "people stayed there all night that
first night, singing and praying," and Coretta Scott King recalled the
times mass meetings ended, "after Martin's message, with a song and
a prayer."[84] Even the police in southern towns seemed to associate the
two acts as being equally unacceptable to their way of thinking. Student
protestors, when taken to jail, were often told by the sheriff, "I don't
want no damn singing and no damn praying."[85] In all of these
comments, activists suggested that the old songs were bound up with a
spiritual part of their lives that had, perhaps, lain dormant before they
became involved in the movement.

Activists spoke of the role of spirituality in much the same way they talked about the emotion generated by the songs. They described their movement away from a detached, intellectual attitude regarding their struggle and advocated a more emotional, spiritual, and complete involvement. When they sang, they claimed they gave themselves fully, gave all they had, to the cause. To argue that the songs were related to the religious or spiritual was to create a subtle willingness to bring to the singing, and the movement, the zeal and commitment one would bring to a religious cause.

This return to a strong sense of spirituality was not necessarily a return to southern versions of Christianity, however. Often the younger activists, in particular, seemed to respond to the spirituality inherent in the religious songs, rather than to the religiosity. For example, while in Mississippi for the voter registration drives, one young activist described the feelings the songs evoked as follows:

> There is almost a religious quality about some of these songs, having little to do with the usual concept of a god. It has to do with the miracle that youth has organized to fight hatred and ignorance. It has to do with the holiness of the dignity of man. The god that makes such miracles is the god I do believe in when we sing "God is on our side." I know I am on that god's side. And I do hope he is on ours.[86]

By their emphasis on emotionalism and spirituality, the activists implied that, to be successful, they must heighten these feelings in themselves and in those who became involved in the movement. They argued that blacks had, at one time, been more willing to indulge their emotional sides and that they should be encouraged to do so again. Because of the nature of the old songs and the behavior associated with singing them, the activists implied that the return to singing of the traditional songs would facilitate an emotional and spiritual commitment to their goals. They suggested the traditional songs imbued them with a special power, associated with the emotion and spirituality inherent in the tradition.

INDIVIDUAL AND COLLECTIVE INVOLVEMENT

Singing was crucial to the activists' success in the movement in that it also provided an unbeatable way to create a sense of community or *esprit de corps*.[87] Activists could easily have sung their songs in solitude, to achieve some of the inspirational benefits of singing, but they knew that, to succeed, they must build and sustain relationships with others.

Scholars argue that oppressors succeed when they are able to isolate and divide those they would oppress. Conversely, resistance to oppression depends largely upon the ability of members of submerged groups to create and maintain a sense of community. Paulo Freire contended, for instance, that a group that seeks to oppress another "cannot permit itself the luxury of tolerating the unification of the people, which would undoubtedly signify a serious threat to their own hegemony."[88] George Rawick added that "people do not individually resist in any significant degree without some sort of support and social confirmation from a community."[89] Many elements of the civil rights struggle, as well as the actions of whites in response to movement activities, had the effect of creating divisions among activists. Singing became a key strategy for counteracting such divisions.

The success or failure of the civil rights movement depended on the drawing together of African Americans in support of the cause. The movement could proceed only if large numbers of people were strongly committed to the ideals of civil rights and the nonviolent philosophy. The nature of the movement and its goals made the task of movement leaders a difficult one.

Unlike many other protest movements where participants are relatively homogeneous, drawn together by occupation, class, or ideology, the civil rights movement drew adherents from virtually all ages and walks of life. Race was the common bond, not education, wealth, or political leaning (and even then, so many white people lent support to the movement that even race may not be seen as a true unifier.) The movement was strengthened by this broad-based appeal, but the diversity also created certain constraints.

Undeniably, factions developed within the civil rights movement, the members of which believed that the endstate of racial equality and freedom should be reached by varying means. All seemed to understand, however, that the factions must be able to work together on some level, and that undue divisiveness would be as debilitating as the resistance offered by outside adversaries.

The songs that made up much of the repertoire of the civil rights activists were group participation songs, the song form most commonly used throughout the history of black song in America. These traditional songs were performed, not by a solo artist playing for the listening enjoyment of others, but by all the members of the group. The freedom songs were designed to be sung by all of the people present at a mass meeting and often took the form of the call and response style traditional in much black singing.

Call and response singing occurs when a singer calls out a line and the rest of the group responds, repeating the line in a stock verse form or responding with a standard chorus. The singer who calls the first line then often drops back to join the large group, while another individual introduces the next line. The style is spontaneous, with no set leader. The members of the singing group, usually all of the people present at a meeting or march, work separately and together, shifting roles, to build the communication. This working together, to co-create a beautiful product, is certainly a means of building a sense of community.

The participants in the civil rights movement talked a great deal about the ways that singing enabled them to unify protesters in ways no other form of communication could. The references to song building unity are too numerous to include here but representative examples are informative. Cordell Reagon argued that "music was what held the movement together," while Sam Block realized after one meeting "how much those songs I had learned, those freedom songs, could help pull us together." For Block, the songs constituted "an organizational glue."[90]

Other activists remarked on the unifying affect of singing as well. Jane Stembridge recalled that when she heard "We Shall Overcome" for the first time, at the first organized student meeting at Shaw University in 1960, "students had just come in from all over the South, meeting for the first time. There was no SNCC, no funds, just people releasing their common vision in that song."[91] According to the activists, their singing was a communication strategy providing them with a quick and effective way of creating group cohesion.

In addition to creating unity among the college students and others who were initially drawn to the movement, it was necessary for activists to involve as many other people as possible and to encourage them to feel an active commitment to the goals of the movement. It is axiomatic that one way to encourage commitment to a goal is to encourage people to voice their support, that once a person has articulated what he or she believes, they are more likely to act accordingly. And yet, the activists understood that many of the people they needed to reach, including the unlettered and unworldly blacks of the rural South, would be easily intimidated by college students and articulate black leaders. Faced with the need to attract and involve people from diverse backgrounds, the activists turned to traditional song because of their strongly held belief in the capacity of this strategy to bridge the gaps between the different peoples.

Activists described singing as a valuable way for young and old and rich and poor to communicate with each other. The songs were called "a basic and common language between organizers who were middle-class Black college students and older adult members of a Black Belt rural area."[92] Reagon remembered the campaign in Albany, Georgia, and the 760 people who were arrested in December of 1961. She said, "the jails were packed with Blacks from all levels of society. . . . One medium of unity and communication with such a group was the songs."[93]

Songs became the way, the activists said, for the civil rights workers to gain a "basic introduction to the communities in which they worked"[94] and to minimize the differences between them and the people they recruited. Lester made this argument about the value of the singing, saying:

> Not only do the songs help to keep the people "marching up to freedom land"; they serve to crumble the class barriers within the Negro community. The professor and the plumber, the society matron and the cleaning woman, the young college student and the unlettered old man stand beside each other, united by a song and a dream.[95]

Like Lester, Reagon suggested that the differences between people vanished when their voices were joined in song, saying, "I would start a song and everyone would join in. After the song, the differences between us would not be as great. Somehow, making a song required an expression that was common to us all."[96] The language choices made by both Lester and Reagon indicated the extent to which they believed singing was capable of uniting diverse people. Reagon said that the "differences between us would not *be* as great." Although the more common usage is probably to say that "differences would not *seem* as great," Reagon's choice of words suggests singing actually removed the differences rather than just making them seem less important. Lester, too, described the removal, rather than the overcoming, of class barriers when he said that singing served to "crumble" such barriers. Music was represented by the activists as a great equalizer. Singing did not simply allow people of different classes and backgrounds to communicate—it made them equal.

In their desire to include blacks from all backgrounds in movement activities, activists argued that they all had the desire to make their voices heard, and that the success of the movement depended on them doing so. The traditional songs provided them with the vehicle to realize this end. SNCC field secretary Charles Jones represented the singing of traditional songs as the way for the common person to be heard, saying that such people "are not articulate. But through songs, they expressed years of suppressed hope, suffering, even joy and love."[97] Lester worried about song writing becoming the domain only of professionals because, he said, this would take song away from the people who needed it most. He argued that "this shouldn't be. The bus driver and the student, the waitress and the secretary, the housewives and businessmen should express themselves. Nor should it stop there; as somebody has said 'Freedom is everybody's business.'"[98] The organizers of the movement claimed that singing was well-suited to their needs because the songs were familiar and comfortable to the masses of people they sought to involve in the movement. They also argued that the songs encouraged those people to comment on their situation.

The songs drew people to movement participation who may have been put off by more confrontational modes of direct action. Taking part in the singing provided those people who were, for whatever reasons, unable to risk going to jail with a way to act and to be involved in the movement. Because every individual in the movement took part in the singing, every individual was part of the action. They were a part of the social act that was the civil rights movement.

The inclusion of music as a rhetorical strategy enabled blacks of all walks of life and all levels of learning to participate in the movement by taking part in an activity with which they already were familiar and comfortable. All participants, whether illiterate rural blacks or young college students, could sing the songs of the movement drawing on lifetimes of experience in expressing themselves through song.

For all that the singing did to enable activists to build a strong sense of community among themselves, it should be understood that the civil rights activists were not simply members of a faceless mass, all unthinkingly moving toward the same goal. Singing encouraged individual, as well as collective involvement, in the movement, and individual identity and responsibility were stressed. As we shall see, the lyrics of many songs stressed the importance of the individual as well as the vital role of the cohesive group. The form of singing complemented the words.

Just as the call and response style of singing built a sense of a community working together to create a song, the individuality of the participants is also stressed in this style of singing. While simple choral singing might downplay the individual voice, call and response allowed individuals to move to the forefront, briefly, and lead the group, before dropping back and letting another singer lead. Separate voices were featured, in their distinctive styles, as described by Josh Dunson:

> The variety of styles was overwhelming. In the song "This Little Light of Mine," five, six, seven or eight leaders would introduce verses that were from their communities. Betty Mae Fikes of Selma, Alabama, whose voice is steel, set the pace with the clapping of her hands: "Up and down this street Lord, I'm going to let it shine." Sam Block of Mississippi belted out "Every time I'm bleeding I'm going to let it shine." Dock Reese sang: "Voting for my Freedom, I'm going to let it shine. Let it shine. Let it shine."[99]

Each singer contributed a strength unique to themselves, something only they could bring, as they cooperatively built the song.

Julius Lester also described the call and response style singing in the civil rights movement, and he, too, stressed how it involved individuals and simultaneously acted to draw those individuals together and to build unity among them:

> Everyone knows what a hard struggle it's been. . . . They don't need anyone to sing to them, because each of them has a song in his own soul. It might take a song leader to pull the beginning of this song from them. But once the collective voice begins to sing, there is no need for a leader. A new verse will be heard down front. New harmony will come from the rear. Somebody will substitute "freedom" for "Jesus" in a verse. The name of the local police chief will be substituted somewhere else. There is never an attempt to sing the songs "right," because the songs are not ends in themselves. They are merely the way in which the community expresses what has happened to its people, what is happening and what, they hope, will eventually happen if they keep up their courage.[100]

Dunson and Lester stressed the individual experience and the individual contribution to the communal recreation of the song while they also invite us to see how such participation inevitably drew people together.

Reagon, too, focused attention on "the one and the many" when she described the participatory singing:

> Black American choral song style is the union of songleader and congregation; the commitment of the singers, masters of their tradition, to speak both individually and in one voice. It is an outstanding example of the unity of group statements existing in total communion with the sanctity of individual expression.[101]

The extent to which these activists stressed their use of song to maintain this tenuous balance of individual and group is consistent with the other principles they held about communication in the movement. They argued that all people had equal right and desire to be heard, but that the communication outlets many of us rely on, speaking and writing, were unavailable or unacceptable to them, so they turned to singing instead.

TRANSFORMATION

As fully as the activists came to believe in the appropriateness of the traditional songs and the traditional way of singing them, so, too, did they believe it was important for them to adapt the songs to better suit the needs of the contemporary struggle. They talked a great deal about the changes made in the songs. Reverend C.T. Vivian acknowledged that it "wasn't just to have the music, but to take the music out of our past and apply it to the new situation, to change it so it really fit."[102] According to Reagon, the accomplished songleader possessed the "fine art of knowing what song to sing at which occasion, when it was necessary to change lyrics, and when songs could be used as they had existed for years in the Black community."[103] Sam Block knew the importance of changing the songs, and passed his knowledge on to others. He remembered that, as a way of involving others he "started to give people the responsibility of thinking about a song that they would want to sing that night and of changing that song."[104] Activists sought an amalgam of old and new, songs of their heritage and of their own creation, to fully express their thoughts and feelings about civil rights.

In many of the references to change appearing in the commentary, activists referred to the simple word changes or verses they added to adapt the old songs to contemporary needs. Reagon remembered how the "new moved from the old in the midst of Movement activity. This evolutionary process was possible because the structure of the traditional material enabled it to function in contemporary settings."[105] The singers referred to their repertoire of old songs as a "storehouse" or "reservoir" from which songleaders drew "to make a new music for a changed time."[106] Their argument for a return to the traditional songs and strategies occurred only in this context of moving forward.

Because song had been such an important element in black lives for so long, the activists in the civil rights movement came to represent it as a life-force in that struggle, implying that, by changing the songs, they could change their lives. In their language choices, activists further represented song as the essential element of the movement activity when they often couched their ideas in terms of a biological or organic metaphor. The activists repeatedly referred to their "growth,"[107] "rooted" in the singing of old songs, which were the "bed of everything."[108]

Reagon described her act of beginning a song in a mass meeting as the "planting of a seed," and Lester described the body of freedom songs as "the rain from a storm, wearing away rocks that bar the way, nourishing dry ground and feeding the seed of freedom."[109] Cotton, too, spoke of the nourishment that comes from song.[110] The songs gave "sustenance" to the singers, were the "heart" and the "soul" of the movement, a "lifeline" for singers, and they, themselves, "came to life" in the singing.[111] The singing was "as natural as daylight," so essential that "the movement without songs would have been like birds without wings."[112] In fact, singing was so closely associated with life that Reagon claimed it was only with the end of life that the singing would stop, saying "they would have to kill us to stop us from singing."[113] For the activists, the act of singing was a vital process; the singers gave voice to the songs and brought them to life and the songs, conversely, provided the activists with the chance to grow and flourish.

The activists' comments about the freedom songs formed an implicit argument defining the songs as a special kind of discourse that was *transformative* in nature. In other words, the songleaders asserted that song aided in the symbolic transformation of the people. By adopting a form of communication that had long been important to blacks in America and by then making positive changes in that communicative form, the activists believed they brought about related positive changes in themselves.

The activists represented their singing in ways emphasizing direct correlations between the changes they made in the song lyrics and the changes they saw occurring in themselves. Reagon attested that "it appeared that songs went through lyrical changes when the protestors needed to affirm their commitment in face of immediate signs to the contrary,"[114] such affirmation constituting a change—a reinforcing or bolstering of commitment.

The activists associated the changes they made in the songs, for instance, with corresponding changes in their ability to remain disciplined and committed in response to intimidation from white officials. Bernice Reagon recounted such a confrontation at a voter registration meeting in 1962:

> The Negroes began to sing. Voices that were weak at first gained strength as they moved up the scale with the old familiar words:
>
> We are climbing Jacob's ladder . . .
>
> Every round goes higher, higher . . .

She continued:

> Now the old sheriff of Terrell County came to the front of the Mount Olive Church. "We want our colored people to live like they've been living," he said. "There was never any trouble before all this started." As he spoke, the whites moved through the church, confronting little groups of Negroes. . . . The Negroes began to sing the strains of another old Baptist hymn, one with some new words and some old, the rising anthem of the whole movement, "We Shall Overcome."[115]

Guy Carawan described a similar situation at Highlander between members of a freedom workshop and local police. He stressed the apprehension experienced by the activists as the police "forced the people—some of them students—to sit in the dark while they went through rooms and searched suitcases and bags." In Carawan's account, the situation changed when someone began to hum "We Shall Overcome." He said:

> Then from a Negro girl—a high school student from Montgomery, Alabama—a new verse came into being. Sitting there in the dark, this girl began to sing, "We are not afraid, we are not afraid today."[116]

It was, according to Carawan, the introduction of a new, especially relevant verse to an old, beloved song that provided the impetus for change within the singers. As the song was changed, so did the singers change, insofar as they felt better equipped to face their fear and overcome it. By drawing on their songs, a combination of the best of the old and new traditions, blacks claimed they were able to stand firm when confronted by white pressure and intimidation tactics.

Reagon remembered other times as well when songs were introduced or changed in response to specific hardships. She wrote of the protestors' actions in Birmingham:

> One of the most dynamic songs out of Birmingham came as a result of the use of dogs and fire hoses by Bull Connor, the visible symbol of the unleashed wrath of white segregationists. This song stated that the use of dogs, fire hoses, and jails would not alter the goals of the marchers.

> > Ain scared of your dogs
> > Cause I want my Freedom
> > I want my Freedom
> > I want my Freedom
> > Ain scared of your dogs
> > Cause I want my freedom
> > I want my freedom now.[117]

Each of these instances of singing was described as a response to a crisis situation and, in the telling, the activists focused on the singing of old/new songs while also stressing the protestors' developing ability to meet the threats of whites without fear and with dignity. This tempering process, the return from confrontation with increased strength, was a recurring theme in the activists' descriptions of movement activity. And, repeatedly, the activists indicated it was song that enabled them to confront and grow stronger.

There is no doubt that the activists believed that when they sang, "a transformation took place inside of people."[118] The changes "inside of people" were manifested in several ways related to the activists' growing ability to respond positively to the adversity they faced in their struggle for equality. Although some of the changes in the songs and the people were small ones, they would lead to larger ones, according to Cordell Reagon:

> The music doesn't change governments. Some bureaucrat or some politician isn't going to be changed by some music he hears. But we can change people—individual people. The people can change governments.[119]

The activists submitted that the changes that were necessary for blacks to undergo were available to them when they sang.

SINGING AND OTHER AUDIENCES

While the songs of the civil rights movement were primarily self-addressed, providing self-definition and direction for the activists who sang the songs, the songs were also heard by people outside the movement membership who, for varying reasons, were concerned about the activists and their world. The choice made by activists to couch much of their public communication in the form of song also had an impact on how these external audiences perceived the activists and their goals.

The people least likely to be moved by the messages in the song—the adversaries of the movement, southern bigots and segregationists—composed one audience for the songs, although the activists did not address them directly and did not explicitly seek a response from their adversaries. Erving Goffman, in his book, *Presentation of Self in Everyday Life*, described the role of the "non-person," and provided a viewpoint to understand how the activists may have targeted their adversaries with their singing, without seeming to do so.

Goffman defined the role of "non-person" as the person who is present during an interaction, but is in the role of neither speaker nor audience.[120] The most telling aspect of this non-person role, for our interests, is that a group can "treat an individual as if he were not present, doing this not because it is the natural thing to do, but as a pointed way of expressing hostility to an individual who has conducted himself improperly."[121] During the civil rights movement, the activists often seemed to cast their adversaries in the role of non-persons. Their singing was not explicitly directed to these people, for it seldom addressed the adversaries or made demands of them. Yet the cooperation of these adversaries was sometimes needed, in a paradoxical way, in order for the activists to accomplish an important goal—to encourage neutral or uninformed observers to align their sympathies with the civil rights activists.

In addition to communicating among themselves regarding their abilities to remain in control, firm in their commitment to nonviolence, the participants in the civil rights movement communicated to those outside the movement, both observers and adversaries, regarding their control. The act of singing suggested a degree of organization and gave the impression of masses of people working together to produce the message. This organization, and the related avoidance of violent behavior, contradicted those who might seek to dismiss the activists as a random group of malcontents and rabble-rousers. Such a presentation of self focused attention on the nonthreatening, peaceful goals of the movement and invited observers to interpret the acts of civil rights participants in a positive way.

The activists also consciously sought to create situations in which observers would be invited to see a strong contrast between the actions of blacks, who strove to appear controlled, polite, law-abiding, and peaceful, and those of white bigots, whose tactics appeared especially heinous when juxtaposed with black nonviolence. Just such a contrast was accomplished during the sit-ins, causing one observer to comment in an editorial in *The Richmond News Leader*, a segregationist paper, in February, 1960:

> Many a Virginian must have felt a tinge of wry regret at the state of things as they are, in reading of Saturday's "sit-downs" by Negro students in Richmond stores. Here were the colored students in coats, white shirts, ties, and one of them was reading Goethe and one was taking notes from a biology text. And here, on the sidewalk outside, was a gang of white boys come to heckle, a ragtail rabble, slack-jawed, black-jacketed, grinning fit to kill. . . . *Eheu!* It gives one pause.[122]

The "tinge of regret" suggests that the writer, perhaps unwillingly, was beginning to question his stereotypes or, at least, was beginning to understand that such a contrast had the power to influence the thinking of other observers.

The choice to sing as a way of communicating among themselves provided activists with a distinctive form of communication, and offered another means by which they could set themselves apart from their adversaries. The singing of the freedom songs was a potent way for activists to highlight the differences between the two groups. Although the white segregationists were not an audience for the messages couched in the songs, the symbolic act of singing influenced them to respond in certain ways that ultimately may have worked to the benefit of the activists.

The nonviolent strategy of protest depends, in part, on activists successfully maintaining a pacifist attitude in the face of violence against them, a stance that may provoke adversaries to increased aggression. By their violent actions against nonviolent protestors, the opponents of a movement reveal themselves as prone to brutality, engaging in it even without overt provocation. Such a confrontation creates a sharp contrast between activists and their opponents, with the controlled and nonviolent actors making a favorable impression on observers. Turner explained this strategy:

> Nonviolence tends to be adopted as movement strategy when adherence to nonviolence facilitates a coalition with a third group against the target group or facilitates a favorable view in a larger public to which the target group is responsive.[123]

This strategy had the potential for great effectiveness during the civil rights movement. Many aspects of the movement were reported by the mass media and, by using a strategy that provided them with a nonviolent, expressive outlet, the civil rights activists created a situation inviting observers, all Americans who were ignorant of or ambivalent about the civil rights movement, to choose between identifying with restrained, controlled persons, singing religious songs, or identifying with their extreme opposites—white bigots willing to turn fire hoses and police dogs on black women and children whose only apparent transgression was singing in the streets.

The act of singing in the civil rights movement, as it was a part of the nonviolent stance of the activists, helped create a radical dichotomy between the acts of the protestors and the acts of the police and segregationists, which cast the latter in such a negative light that many Americans, given the choice, felt they *must* sympathize with the civil rights participants. Bayard Rustin commented on this reaction of observers who responded only when faced with specific, unarguable examples of brutality, saying that blacks "gained moral authority not because Americans opposed segregation, but because black people were suffering, because churches were bombed and children firehosed."[124] In their conviction that it would take just such scenes to awaken the average American to the situation in the South, civil rights activists made use of the strategy of song, and other manifestations of nonviolent direct action, to heighten the differences between their actions and those of their adversaries.

The related issue of petitioning is a relevant one in the discussion of the civil rights movement and the ways that activists engaged "non-persons" to help them reach their goals. Todd Gitlin, writing about the Student New Left during the 1960s and 1970s, noted that the protestors were always at a disadvantage, whether dealing with the press, with the police, or with other authorities who stood in the way of change. This disadvantage resulted from the students' role as *petitioners*, as people who could act in aggressive ways but who nonetheless were reliant on getting others, their adversaries, to cooperate with them. Gitlin provided an example of this reliance when he wrote of the activists' strategy of getting arrested. He said:

> But not even the activists bent on arrests for publicity's sake can get arrested unless the police authorities *decide* to make the arrests. (Even the grammar of the passive voice shows that the activists remain passive in the situation: they must *get* arrested.)[125]

The student activists had little control over the situations that they wished to change, most notably the continuance of the Vietnam war. They used their symbolic acts to draw attention to their cause but they were continually faced with asking for help from the very people who were supporting the war effort.

In contrast, the activists in the civil rights movement were much less dependent on outside cooperation for the accomplishment of certain of their goals. It would be unrealistic to claim that blacks were entirely unconcerned with the cooperation of whites, though. The strategy of nonviolence is designed, in part, to provoke adversaries to react violently and to reveal the worst of themselves. Had whites failed to cooperate and react as expected, the nature of the movement as a whole would have been changed. (In fact, at least one southern lawman attempted, and succeeded to some degree, to respond nonviolently to nonviolence. Laurie Pritchett, police chief of Albany, Georgia, learned what he could of nonviolent philosophy and tactics and directed his police officers to "out-nonviolent" the activists when they came to town. Opinions vary as to the success of this strategy, but most civil rights leaders saw the Albany campaign as somewhat disappointing).[126]

Blacks also used arrests as a strategy, in the way described by Gitlin, and such use may seem to place the civil rights activists in the position of the student New Left—as dependent on their adversaries. This was true to a certain extent, as Howard Zinn made evident when quoting from a letter written by a civil rights activist in Atlanta. The activist wrote in language very similar to Gitlin's and stressed the extent to which the civil rights activists were using the arrests as a strategy:

> To date there are 82 students and tomorrow all hell should break loose as the ministers are going to sit-in and be arrested, if Captain Jenkins continues to cooperate with us.[127]

It must be clear that, in such a situation as this, blacks relied upon, and very often got, certain kinds of cooperation from whites. The leaders of the movement understood this dependence and learned that it could be used as a tool.

In spite of the obvious similarities in the interactions between both the civil rights and New Left activists and their adversaries, there was a crucial difference as well. While the New Left activists were entirely dependent on the cooperative responses of their adversaries, the civil rights activists retained a great deal of control. In their protest against the Vietnam War, the New Left could not make personal changes that would have any direct effect on the war. The civil rights activists, in contrast, could change their situation by changing themselves.

Just as the opponents of the civil rights movement can be considered an audience of sorts for the freedom songs, the singing communicated to ambivalent whites outside the movement as well. Here again, activists did not specifically address this group in their singing, but the singers seemed to recognize the potential for their message to be "overheard." The songs carried information about human being and social action to people outside the movement ranks.

When communication takes place in a public arena, it is likely that it will reach listeners beyond the in-group for whom it is ostensibly designed. The civil rights songs were, indeed, often sung in the public arena. Voices were raised not only in the black churches and in the jails, but on the streets. This public communication attracted the attention of the media who then carried the songs to much larger audiences. The songs received serious coverage in such popular magazines as *Newsweek, The New Yorker, U. S. News and World Report*, and *The Saturday Review*, where reporters drew white attention to the civil rights music as "a source of strength, unification, and expression."[128] The extent to which the civil rights movement was covered by the broadcast media also meant that the sights and sounds of black protest reached a great many white Americans.

This likelihood that whites would "overhear" the songs of black civil rights activists meant that the activists' communication had the potential to influence those overhearers and their perceptions of the movement. James Carey's thoughts on a ritual view of communication are useful in understanding the way the freedom songs may have communicated to movement outsiders.

Carey argued that a ritual view of communication is more appropriate for studying communication than the widely accepted transmission view.[129] The ritual view shifts attention from communication as a process of transmitting and acquiring information to an understanding of communication as dramatic action, wherein listeners are invited to participate in the drama represented by the communication. In Carey's judgment, this view:

> sees the original and highest manifestation of communication not in the transmission of intelligent information but in the construction and maintenance of an ordered, meaningful cultural world that can serve as a control and container for human action.[130]

In other words, communication serves less to persuade or to teach than to frame perceptions and build community.

In discussing the freedom songs of the civil rights movement, we can seek to understand how the singers represented reality and social interaction, rather than to try to discover how the songs *informed* listeners. The songs were not an overt persuasive appeal, asking listeners to make a choice between the status quo and supporting the civil rights movement. Instead, the singers provided a representation of themselves and their struggle that cast listeners into the role of movement supporters.

For the "overhearers," the act of singing carried information regarding the sense of being held by blacks and of the potential relationship between blacks and whites. Whites were subtly invited to share the new definition of self blacks were shaping and were also invited to see themselves as cooperative agents in the changes in the South.

By choosing to couch their goals in the songs of the religion fundamental to much of white American culture, blacks subtly associated their hopes with white hopes. The familiar musical forms and themes of the activists' traditional Christian songs highlighted common ground in the experiences and goals of blacks and whites.

The music of the civil rights songs was not strongly based on the rhythms and special sounds of African or African American music, styles that might be so unfamiliar as to alienate white American listeners of the 1960s. The traditional songs of the activists' repertoire were marked more by Western influences than were many other forms of black music that show strong African American influence. Scholars argue that blacks have often used their music as a way to set themselves apart from whites rather than as a way to build alliances.[131] The blues are black, soul is black, jazz is black, and the slave spirituals were inherently black, although there is a related genre of the white spiritual, from which some scholars argue the black songs derived. The songs chosen by civil rights activists were black songs as well, but they seemed to highlight less strongly the differences between black and white than do the many other song forms available to activists. The songs were rooted in black tradition, so they spoke to the activists regarding their heritage as Africans, but they were also indelibly marked with the American religious tradition and with Western musical patterns, so the songs communicated to activists and observers regarding their shared American heritage as well.

SUMMARY

The remainder of this book comprises an analysis of the lyrics of the freedom songs, as those lyrics constitute a positive self-definition for the singers. In that analysis, it is always important to remember that the freedom songs were *songs,* and that singing, as such, played an important role in the movement. Nowhere was it foreordained that the activists had to sing, that they had to sing songs from black tradition, that they had to sing together, that they had to sing in call and response style as they often did, or that they had to sing, frequently, in public settings where people outside the civil rights vanguard would have access to the songs.

The choices the activists made were crucial to the power and appeal of their communication. The self-definition created by the activists began with the decision to sing, a decision that defined them as closely bound to their ancestors, and as appreciative of their heritage and the emotionalism and spirituality attendant to it. They also created, as they sang, a balance in their self-definition between their reliance on and commitment to the group and their individual responsibility. All of these elements of definition were reinforced and amplified by the choices activists made regarding the content of their songs.

NOTES

1. "Without These Songs . . ." *Newsweek*, 31 August 1964, 74.

2. Bob Cohen in Guy Carawan and Candie Carawan, *Freedom is a Constant Struggle* (New York: Oak Publications, 1968), 71; Cordell Reagon in Pete Seeger and Bob Reiser, *Everybody Says Freedom* (New York: W.W. Norton, 1989) 77; John Lewis in Bernice Johnson Reagon, "Songs of the Civil Rights Movement 1955-1965: A Study in Culture History" (Ph.D. diss. Howard University, 1975), 102; Bernice Reagon in Seeger and Reiser, *Everybody Says*, 82; John Lewis in Wayne Hampton, *Guerrilla Minstrels* (Knoxville: University of Tennessee Press, 1986), 58; Cordell Reagon in Seeger and Reiser, *Everybody Says*, 85; Wyatt Tee Walker in Guy Carawan and Candie Carawan, *We Shall Overcome: Songs of the Southern Freedom Movement* (New York: Oak Publications, 1963), 11; unidentified activist in David King Dunaway, *How Can I Keep From Singing: Pete Seeger* (New York: Da Capo, 1981), 223; James Farmer, *Lay Bare the Heart: An Autobiography of the Civil Rights Movement* (New York: Arbor, 1985), 7.

3. Carawan and Carawan, *We Shall Overcome*, 7.

4. Bob Cohen in Carawan and Carawan, *Freedom*, 71.

5. Wyatt Tee Walker in Carawan and Carawan, *We Shall Overcome*, 11.

6. Candie Anderson Carawan in Carawan and Carawan, *We Shall Overcome*, 18.

7. Pat Watters, *Down To Now: Reflections on the Southern Civil Rights Movement* (New York: Random, 1971), 180.

8. Reagon, "Songs of the Civil Rights Movement," 127-128.

9. Cordell Reagon in Watters, *Down To Now*, 21; Charles Jones in Reagon, "Songs of the Civil Rights Movement," 138.

10. James R. Irvine and Walter G. Kirkpatrick, "The Musical Form in Rhetorical Exchange: Theoretical Considerations," *Quarterly Journal of Speech* 58 (1972), 272-3.

11. Euvester Simpson in Kay Mills, *This Little Light of Mine: The Life of Fannie Lou Hamer* (New York: Dutton, 1993), 60.

12. Howard Zinn, *SNCC: The New Abolitionists*, 2nd ed. (Boston: Beacon, 1965), 131.

13. Bob Cohen in Reagon, "Songs of the Civil Rights Movement," 152.

14. Reagon, "Songs of the Civil Rights Movement," 139.

15. Unidentified activist in Elizabeth Sutherland, ed., *Letters from Mississippi* (New York: McGraw-Hill, 1965), 50.

16. Josh Dunson, *Freedom in the Air: Song Movements of the Sixties* (New York: International, 1965), 67.

17. Bernice Johnson Reagon in Henry Hampton and Steve Fayer, *Voices of Freedom: An Oral History of the Civil Rights Movement from the 1950s through the 1980s* (New York: Bantam, 1990), 108; Willie Peacock in Seeger and Reiser, *Everybody Says*, 180.

18. Bernice Johnson Reagon, "In Our Hands: Thoughts on Black Music," *Sing Out!*, November 1975, 2.

19. Ben Sidran, *Black Talk* (New York: Holt, Rinehart & Winston, 1971), 1-29.

20. John Lovell, Jr., *Black Song: The Forge and the Flame* (New York: MacMillan, 1972), 42.

21. Gerhard Putschogl, "Black Music--Key Force in Afro-American Culture: Archie Shepp on Oral Tradition and Black Culture," in *History and Tradition in Afro-American Culture*, ed. Gunter H. Lenz (Frankfurt: Campus Verlag, 1984), 264.

22. Lovell, *Black Song*, 37.

23. Lawrence Levine, *Black Culture and Black Consciousness* (New York: Oxford University Press, 1972), 8-19.

24. Chopi maxim, in Lovell, *Black Song*, 7.

25. Mintz and Price, qtd. in Christopher Small, *Music of the Common Tongue: Survival and Celebration in Afro-American Music* (New York: River Run, 1987), 34.

26. I. Ira Goldenberg, *Oppression and Social Intervention* (Chicago: Nelson, 1978), 2-3. See also Goldenberg, *Oppression*, 48; Paulo Freire, *Pedagogy of the Oppressed*, trans. Myra Bergman Ramos (New York: Continuum, 1984), 49-50, 151; Herbert Aptheker, *American Negro Slave Revolts*. 1943. (New York: International, 1969), 53-55.

27. Hampton and Fayer, *Voices of Freedom*, xxiii; Cal Logue, "Rhetorical Ridicule of Reconstruction Blacks," *Quarterly Journal of Speech* 62 (1978), 401.

28. Kenneth Stampp, *The Peculiar Institution* (New York: Knopf, 1967), 145.

29. Stampp, *Peculiar Institution*, 145.

30. James H. Cone, *The Spirituals and the Blues* (New York: Seabury, 1972), 16.

31. Thomas Frederick Jones, "A Rhetorical Study of Black Songs: 1860-1930" (Master's thesis, University of Georgia, Athens, 1973), 20.

32. Jones, "Rhetorical Study of Black Song," 103.

33. Charles Keil, *Urban Blues* (Chicago: University of Chicago Press, 1966), 15; Sidran, *Black Talk*, 33.

34. Sidran, *Black Talk*, 155.

35. Levine, *Black Culture*, 162.

36. Dena Epstein, *Sinful Tunes and Spirituals* (Urbana: University of Illinois Press, 1977), 275.

37. Hampton and Fayer, *Voices of Freedom*, 30.

38. Julius Lester in Dunson, *Freedom in the Air*, 35.

39. Carawan and Carawan, *We Shall Overcome*, 5.

40. Guy Carawan in Dunson, *Freedom in the Air*, 39.

41. Guy Carawan and Candie Carawan, *Sing for Freedom: The Story of the Civil Rights Movement Through Its Songs* (Bethlehem, PA: Sing Out, 1990), 3.

42. Carawan and Carawan, *We Shall Overcome*, 8.

43. Len Chandler in Dunson, *Freedom in the Air*, 1-2.

44. Guy Carawan in Carawan and Carawan, *Freedom*, 71.

45. Bernice Reagon in Juan Williams, *Eyes on the Prize: America's Civil Rights Years, 1954-1965* (New York: Viking, 1987), 163.

46. Bessie Jones in Carawan and Carawan, *Freedom*, 112.

47. Andrew Young in Carawan and Carawan, *Freedom*, 110.

48. Reagon, "Songs of the Civil Rights Movement," 88. See also Dunaway, *Keep From Singing*, 222-223.

49. Lyndon B. Johnson in Hampton and Fayer, *Voices of Freedom*, 235.

50. Williams, *Eyes on the Prize*, 278-279; Reagon, "Songs of the Civil Rights Movement," 175.

51. This reaction of activists ran counter to their stated goal to work "black and white together" and may seem to draw into doubt the civil rights principles of equality and agapic love. It is probably more fair to recognize the activists' reaction as bewilderment—the stance they had taken as their own, of which they felt proud, had perhaps become obsolete. The songs symbolized the dreams and goals of the movement but, in accomplishing what they were designed to accomplish, the songs, it seemed, were no longer necessary. Johnson's words and the passage of the voting rights bill signaled a need for yet more change in

the movement. Much for which the activists had struggled had been accomplished and they were faced with a choice—they could call the civil rights movement a success and end their involvement or they could continue their protests, in a more militant way, claiming they wanted more than they currently had. The activists' reaction to President Johnson's speech probably grew from these complex concerns.

52. Cordell Reagon in "Without These Songs," 74.

53. Reagon, "Songs of the Civil Rights Movement," 29.

54. Reagon, "Songs of the Civil Rights Movement," 109.

55. Carawan and Carawan, *We Shall Overcome*, 8.

56. Julius Lester, "Freedom Songs in the South," *Broadside* 39 (Feb. 7, 1964): 1.

57. In discussing the traditional orientation of the freedom songs, songs derived from a folk tradition, it is important to recognize that traditional music was only one option available to the activists. The presence of music rooted in an oral tradition does *not* indicate that the activists were less intelligent than trained musicians or that they were primitive or illiterate. The participants in the civil rights movement could easily have chosen modes of communication drawing more heavily on the education of the young people, the many college students who gave the movement much of its impetus. Indeed, many genres of black music fall closer to the art end of a continuum between folk and art music and many people in the movement were highly literate and chose to emphasize their intellect, rather than their traditional roots. The songs chosen were not from a folk or oral tradition because they *had* to be. They were of a folk nature because the activists believed that such songs, drawn from their tradition, had a different kind of communicative power than did the other forms of communication available.

58. Bessie Jones in Carawan and Carawan, *Freedom*, 112.

59. Amanda Bowens in Dunson, *Freedom in the Air*, 104.

60. Martin Luther King, Jr., in Reagon, "Songs of the Civil Rights Movement," 15.

61. Reagon, "Songs of the Civil Rights Movement," 107.

62. Levine, *Black Culture*, 184.

63. Mills, *Little Light*, 137.

64. Guy Carawan in Dunson, *Freedom in the Air*, 39.

65. Carawan and Carawan, *We Shall Overcome*, 8.

66. Bernice Reagon in Williams, *Eyes on the Prize*, 177.

67. Charles Sherrod in Zinn, *SNCC*, 128-129.

68. Reagon, "In Our Hands," 1.

69. Bernice Reagon in Seeger and Reiser, *Everybody Says*, 82.

70. Cordell Reagon in Seeger and Reiser, *Everybody Says*, 85.

71. Wyatt Tee Walker in Carawan and Carawan, *We Shall Overcome*, 11; Carawan and Carawan, *We Shall Overcome*, 64; Willie Peacock in Carawan and Carawan, *Freedom*, 140.

72. Cordell Reagon in Watters, *Down To Now*, 21.

73. Hollis Watkins in Seeger and Reiser, *Everybody Says*, 179.

74. Julius Lester in Carawan and Carawan, *We Shall Overcome*, 23; Esau Jenkins in Carawan and Carawan, *Freedom*, 135; Reagon, "Songs of the Civil Rights Movement," 171; Reagon, "In Our Hands," 1; Lester, "Freedom Songs," 1; Reagon, *Voices of the Civil Rights Movement*, 6, 14; Cordell Reagon in Seeger and Reiser, *Everybody Says*, 77.

75. Carawan and Carawan, *We Shall Overcome*, 7; Bernice Reagon, "Let the Church Sing 'Freedom,'" *Black Music Research Journal* 7 (1987), 111.

76. Carawan and Carawan, *We Shall Overcome*, 5, 7; Candie Anderson Carawan in *We Shall Overcome*, 16.

77. Fannie Lou Hamer in Mills, *Little Light*, 21.

78. James Farmer in Hampton and Fayer, *Voices of Freedom*, 95. See also James Farmer, *Lay Bare the Heart*, 27-30.

79. Esau Jenkins in Carawan and Carawan, *Freedom*, 135.

80. Reagon, "Let the Church Sing," 111.

81. Willie Peacock in Seeger and Reiser, *Everybody Says*, 180.

82. Cordell Reagon in Seeger and Reiser, *Everybody Says*, 77.

83. Reagon, "Let the Church Sing," 113; Goldie Jackson in Watters, *Down To Now*, 158.

84. Goldie Jackson in Seeger and Reiser, *Everybody Says*, 72; Coretta Scott King in Hampton and Fayer, *Voices of Freedom*, 30. See also Reagon, "Songs of the Civil Rights Movement," 14; Reagon, "In Our Hands," 1; Willie Peacock in Reagon, "Let the Church Sing," 113; Reagon, *Voices of the Civil Rights Movement*, 6; Bernard Lafayette in Seeger and Reiser, *Everybody Says*, 55; anonymous woman in Watters, *Down to Now*, 238.

85. Carawan and Carawan, *We Shall Overcome*, 62.

86. Heather [Tobis] in Sutherland, *Letters from Mississippi*, 151.

87. For a discussion of the importance of *esprit de corps* to protest, see Herbert Blumer, "Social Movements," in *The Sociology of Dissent*, ed. R. Serge Denisoff, (New York: Harcourt, 1974), 9-11.

88. Freire, *Pedagogy*, 137.

89. George P. Rawick, *From Sundown to Sunup: The Making of the Black Community* (Westport, CN: Greenwood, 1972), 107. See also George M. Fredrickson, and Christopher Lasch, "Resistance to Slavery," in *The Debate Over Slavery: Stanley Elkins and His Critics*, ed. Ann J. Lane (Urbana: University of Illinois Press, 1971), 239; Elizabeth Fox-Genovese, "Strategies and Forms of Resistance: Focus on Slave Women in the United States," in *In Resistance: Studies in African, Caribbean, and Afro-American History*, ed. Gary Y. Okihiro (Amherst: University of Massachusetts Press, 1986), 159.

90. Cordell Reagon in Seeger and Reiser, *Everybody Says*, 85; Sam Block in Seeger and Reiser, *Everybody Says*, 179.

91. Jane Stembridge in Seeger and Reiser, *Everybody Says*, 36.

92. Reagon, "Songs of the Civil Rights Movement," 178.

93. Reagon, "Songs of the Civil Rights Movement," 135.

94. Reagon, "Songs of the Civil Rights Movement," 179.

95. Lester, "Freedom Songs," 2.

96. Reagon, "In Our Hands," 1.

97. Charles Jones in Reagon, "Songs of the Civil Rights Movement," 138.

98. Julius Lester in Reagon, "Songs of the Civil Rights Movement," 161.

99. Dunson, *Freedom in the Air*, 101.

100. Lester, "Freedom Songs," 1-2.

101. Reagon, *Voices of the Civil Rights Movement*, 7.

102. Reverend C.T. Vivian in Carawan and Carawan, *Sing for Freedom*, 4.

103. Reagon, "Songs of the Civil Rights Movement," 179-180.

104. Sam Block in Charles M. Payne, *I've Got the Light of Freedom: The Organizing Tradition and the Mississippi Freedom Struggle* (Berkeley: University of California Press, 1995), 147.

105. Reagon, "Songs of the Civil Rights," 96.

106. Reagon, "Let the Church Sing," 106; Reagon, *Voices of the Civil Rights Movement*, 7.

107. Carawan and Carawan, *We Shall Overcome*, 7; Julius Lester in Carawan and Carawan, *We Shall Overcome*, 23; Dorothy Cotton in Carawan and Carawan, *Freedom*, 27.

108. Carawan and Carawan, *Freedom*, 112; Reagon, "Songs of the Civil Rights Movement," 25, 29; Bernice Reagon in Williams, *Eyes on the Prize*, 177.

109. Bernice Reagon in Williams, *Eyes on the Prize*, 177; Lester, "Freedom Songs," 2.

110. Dorothy Cotton, lecture at The Pennsylvania State University, April 4, 1988.

111. Carawan and Carawan, *We Shall Overcome*, 8; John Lewis in Reagon, "Songs of the Civil Rights Movement," 102; Esau Jenkins in Carawan and Carawan, *Freedom*, 135; Guy Carawan in Seeger and Reiser, *Everybody Says*, 39; Reagon, "Let the Church Sing," 106.

112. Cordell Reagon in Seeger and Reiser, *Everybody Says*, 77; John Lewis in Hampton, *Guerilla Minstrels*, 58.

113. Bernice Reagon in Williams, *Eyes on the Prize*, 177.

114. Reagon, "Songs of the Civil Rights Movement," 103.

115. Reagon, "Songs of the Civil Rights Movement," 136-137.

116. Guy Carawan in Reagon, "Songs of the Civil Rights Movement," 82.

117. Reagon, "Songs of the Civil Rights Movement," 148.

118. Bernice Reagon in Williams, *Eyes on the Prize*, 177.

119. Cordell Reagon in Seeger and Reiser, *Everybody Says*, 85.

120. Erving Goffman, *The Presentation of Self in Everyday Life* (New York: Overlook, 1973), 151.

121. Goffman, *Presentation of Self*, 153.

122. Watters, *Down To Now*, 97.

123. Turner, "Determinants," 162.

124. Bayard Rustin, *Strategies for Freedom: The Changing Patterns of Black Protest* (New York: Columbia University Press, 1976), 24.

125. Todd Gitlin, *The Whole World is Watching: Mass Media in the Making and Unmaking of the New Left* (Berkeley: University of California Press, 1980), 43.

126. See Laurie Pritchett in Howell Raines, *My Soul Is Rested: Movement Days in the Deep South Remembered* (New York: Penguin, 1977), 361-366; Payne, *Light of Freedom*, 394.

127. Howard Zinn, *The Southern Mystique* (New York: Knopf, 1964), 135.

128. Burt Korall, "The Music of Protest," *Saturday Review,* November, 1968, 37. See also "Moment of History," *New Yorker* 27 March 1965, 37-39; "Without These Songs," 74; "Battle Hymn of the Integrationists," *U.S. News and World Report* 5 August 1963, 8.

129. James W. Carey, *Communication as Culture: Essays on Media and Society* (Boston: Unwin Hyman, 1989), 18-23.

130. Carey, *Communication as Culture,* 18-19.

131. Robert Francesconi, "Free Jazz and Black Nationalism: A Rhetoric of Musical Style," *Critical Studies in Mass Communication* 3 (1986): 36-49.

III

"We Shall All Be Free":
The Activists' Goal and Self-Definition

The words of the civil rights songs provide an eloquent text for gaining knowledge to the movement and the people behind it. As noted, the activists chose to sing songs from the black music tradition, and adapted these songs to combine the traditional words with updated, local references. A detailed look at the words of the songs, and the ways the activists described themselves and their undertaking, provides us with special insight to the movement, from the point of view of the people who initiated it.

The activists of the civil rights movement were engaged in seeking change in the status quo in their own lives and in the United States. To direct their energies, the activists needed a sense of the future—what goal or motivation made the future promising for them? Who would they *be* in the changed world they sought? What, specifically, would that world entail? By what actions could they achieve the desired changes? The songs of the civil rights movement provided this view of the future for the activists. As they sang their freedom songs, they offered among themselves definitions of the changes they would undergo and they would bring about in their world.

THE ACTIVISTS' GOAL: "OH FREEDOM"

An important question to ask of any movement is What do the protestors want? What exactly do they see as their goal? Only by answering such questions can we appreciate and analyze the strategies undertaken by activists in pursuit of that goal. During the civil rights movement, activists responded to a wide variety of perceived injustices and mistreatments but, according to the songs they sang, they defined their primary motivation not as equality, equal rights, justice, or even civil rights.

The activists' primary goal was "freedom," the theme that dominated their singing. That the songs sung at every movement activity were commonly referred to by movement members as "freedom songs" provides the first bit of evidence that the activists saw freedom as their primary concern, but a great deal of additional evidence is available as well.

From the first days of the movement, freedom was identified as the objective that inspired activists and made their involvement necessary. In the early days of the Montgomery bus boycott, a cardboard sign provided blacks, in no uncertain terms, with the reason they must refuse to take the buses: "DON'T RIDE THE BUSES TODAY. DON'T RIDE IT FOR FREEDOM."[1] Likewise, during this first sustained protest for civil rights, at the first mass meeting of the Montgomery Improvement Association, participants articulated their goal. Reporter Joe Azbell wrote of the focus on freedom, even at that early stage:

> That audience was so on fire that the preacher would get up and say, "Do you want your freedom?" And they'd say, "Yeah, I want my freedom!" . . . and they were so excited . . . they were on fire for freedom.[2]

When Annell Ponder went to jail, after being beaten by police, Ida Holland remembered what remained in Ponder's thoughts—her face "was swollen and she had a black eye. She could barely talk, but she looked at me and whispered, 'Freedom.'"[3] The identification of freedom as the primary goal of the movement began early and was reinforced, in significant ways, by the freedom songs themselves.

The civil rights songs focused on freedom to an overwhelming extent in ways both explicit and subtle. In such popular freedom songs as "Oh Freedom," "(Everybody Says) Freedom," "Over My Head I See Freedom in the Air," and others, the focus on freedom is obvious and striking. In these songs, activists featured freedom in very straightforward ways as their ultimate goal. Singers asserted that they were "marching up to freedom land"[4] and "on my way to freedom land,"[5] while also describing their search for freedom:

> Jordan's River is deep and wide,
> We'll find freedom on the other side.[6]

They clearly stated "we want freedom here" and affirmed that "we must be free."[7] The singers left little doubt that they were motivated by a dream of true and complete freedom—of the 24 songs under consideration here, 19 included the words the words "freedom" and "free," often in the chorus or other repeated lines, so references to freedom were abundant. By way of comparison, "equality" appeared in two songs, "civil rights" and "voting" in three songs each, "justice" in one, and "integration" in one, with "segregation" identified as undesirable in two more songs.[8]

Just as singers explicitly defined freedom as the goal of the movement, they also more subtly reinforced this claim by referring to freedom in ways that would be likely to draw special attention to the theme. In many of the songs, for instance, the theme of freedom is introduced and highlighted in the first lines sung.

Kenneth Burke, literary and rhetorical critic, advocated that critics give special attention to beginnings and endings of communication messages, as well as to the moments when a change of direction occurs. He asked, "Might there not also be the *qualitative* importance of beginning, middle, and end? That is: should we not attach particular significance to the situations on which the work opens and closes, and the events by which the peripety, or reversal is contrived?"[9] Rhetorical critic Carroll C. Arnold, too, stressed the beginning and end as places of special interest for students of language insofar as the "placement of ideas in relation to one another affects the importance those ideas will have for listeners, the first and final places being those of most significance."[10] Burke and Arnold argued that material presented at the beginnings and endings is given special weight by its placement, making it likely that listeners will attend to that material. Because beginnings and endings are significant in this way, and because they will be perceived as important by listeners, we should be especially interested in these "places," and the clues they provide to understanding a message.

Accordingly, it is significant that several of the freedom songs began by focusing listeners' attention specifically on freedom. "Oh Freedom" and "Woke Up This Morning With My Mind on Freedom" began with specific references to freedom, an initial emphasis that was continually reinforced throughout the songs. The word "freedom" appeared fifteen times in five verses of "Woke Up This Morning With

My Mind on Freedom," leaving little doubt about the activists' preoccupations.

In "Over My Head I See Freedom in the Air," the word "freedom" appeared only three times, all in the first of three verses, but freedom was still clearly the theme of the song. The placement of "freedom" in the first line and verse encouraged listeners to perceive freedom as the focus of the song, and of the movement. Freedom was the subject of the first sentence and, in the metaphor used by activists, freedom was cast as the state that filled the singers' senses and surrounded them.

The choice to sing of freedom first, in "Over My Head I See Freedom in the Air" as well as other songs, also served to frame or index what followed in other verses. In "Over My Head," singers made incremental changes in the words of the verses, substituting "glory" and "victory" for freedom ("Over my head I see glory in the air . . ."). Because these goals were sung of only after freedom had been emphasized as the primary goal, listeners were likely to have seen "glory" and "victory" as related to freedom, but as dependent on it. In other words, singers suggested that the only way their lives could be glorious or that they could be victorious was by becoming fully free.

Freedom was not always mentioned in the first lines or verses of the songs, but the theme was subtly emphasized nonetheless. In "We Shall Not Be Moved," for instance, the activists described their determination to stand firm in the first verse of the song. The verses of the song then served to detail the reasons and motivations for such determination. The first reason the activists gave for why "we shall not be moved" was "we are fighting for our freedom." The desire for freedom determined the behavior of the activists.

In "This Little Light of Mine," "freedom" is not mentioned until the second verse of the song. At that point, though, it becomes clear that the "little light" central to the first verse and bridge is the "light of freedom":

> We've got the light of freedom,
> We're gonna let it shine.

Activists gave concrete meaning to the metaphor of the "little light," defining it, at least in part, as freedom. Freedom, although not mentioned first, was closely associated with the theme that was addressed, a construction likely to encourage listeners to see freedom as important to the thoughts and actions of the activists.

In their linguistic focus on freedom, activists also found ways to introduce the theme early without explicit reference to it. In "Keep Your Eyes on the Prize," for example, freedom was implicitly emphasized in the first verses, as singers retold the biblical story of Paul and Silas, beginning with the lines "Paul and Silas bound in jail/ Had no money to go their bail." Paul and Silas's bondage was soon downplayed, however, as singers moved to the second verse and the moment when "the jail door opened and they walked out." This tale of bondage and freedom set a scene that was more explicitly argued in the third and fourth verses of the song, where singers asserted that "freedom's name is mighty sweet" and "we'll find freedom on the other side." The combination of the biblical narrative describing the achievement of freedom and the direct assertion that freedom was highly appealing and attainable provided two different types of verbal highlighting likely to assure that listeners understood that the quest for freedom was the "prize" that drew activists together.

In "Oh Pritchett, Oh Kelley," activists similarly stressed freedom without using the word. In the first lines of that song, singers pleaded, ostensibly with Albany, Georgia, police chief Laurie Pritchett and Mayor Asa Kelley:

> Oh, Pritchett, Oh, Kelley,
> Oh, Pritchett, open them cells.
> Oh, Pritchett, Oh, Kelley,
> Oh, Pritchett, open them cells.

In this song, as in "Keep Your Eyes on the Prize," the theme of imprisonment was used to emphasize the activists' desire for freedom. These references were made resonant in the civil rights movement when many activists did, in fact, go to jail as part of their strategy of civil disobedience. Bondage and freedom, literal and metaphorical, became entwined in the movement, and these themes appeared often in the activists' songs.

The theme of freedom was subtly highlighted in "We Shall Overcome" as well. One of the two verses that most closely paralleled the chorus "we shall overcome" in terms of structure and language was "we shall all be free." In contrast, other verses varied widely, keeping only the basic metre of the key refrain of the song. For instance, such verses as "black and white together" and "the Lord will see us through" did not correspond as neatly to "we shall overcome" as did other lines that began with "we shall" and maintained the same number of syllables in the line. The parallelisms in "we shall overcome" and "we shall all be free" drew attention to those lines and implicitly argued that "overcoming" was linked to "being free."

The importance of freedom was also advanced insofar as the activists described its pervasiveness in their lives. In the songs, the singers claimed that freedom filled their waking thoughts and motivated their actions. Thoughts of freedom were so compelling that singers could claim "I woke up this morning with my mind on freedom" and suggest that freedom surrounded them: "Over my head I see freedom in the air" and "Oh freedom over me." The desire for freedom also enabled activists to repudiate their fear of the threats used against them, as they sang "Ain't a-scared of your jail 'cause I want my freedom." Freedom was a powerful force in the lives of the singers.

In "Oh Freedom," activists gave great weight and significance to the concept of freedom, with the frequent repetition of the lines:

> And before I'd be a slave,
> I'd be buried in my grave,
> And go home to my Lord and be free

This association between freedom and life itself was featured in "Freedom Is a Constant Struggle" as well. Activists sang:

> They say that freedom is a constant dying,
> They say that freedom is a constant dying,
> They say that freedom is a constant dying,
> Oh Lord, we've died so long,
> We must be free, we must be free.

The words of these song were given added meaning when protestors literally gave their lives in support of the cause. Freedom, in the context of these messages, became more than an abstract goal—it became something for which activists lived and died. Activists defined their commitment as more intense than that usually made by humans, for conventional wisdom would say life is the ultimate gift and, therefore, the ultimate sacrifice. The act of suffering and dying for a cause, and implicitly, for those who would live on and benefit from the cause, placed the singers in the company of other Christian martyrs who put the good of all before their individual worth.

The civil rights activists' focus on freedom is especially evident when the civil rights songs are contrasted with the earlier songs from which they were derived. Some of those songs, like "I'll Be All Right" (the song from which "We Shall Overcome" was derived) and "Oh Freedom," spoke of a desire for freedom even in their earliest versions.[11] More often, however, the emphasis on freedom was added to the songs as activists adapted them for the civil rights movement.

One early version of "We Shall Not Be Moved," for instance, reflects its religious roots, and the singer's focus on personal salvation, rather than on freedom for all African Americans:

I shall not, I shall not be moved,
I shall not, I shall not be moved,
Just like a tree that's planted by the water,
I shall not be moved.

On my way to heaven, I shall not be moved . . .

Fightin' sinnin' Satan . . .

Jesus is my captain . . .[12]

A later version of the song, collected in 1940, suggests the singers' concerns were different both from those of earlier singers and the ones who adopted the songs 20 years later. In the 1940s, the song was sung by laborers in their struggle to organize and build unions. Their version of "We Shall Not Be Moved" referred to their leader and their district president, the people on whom they were relying to help them change their lives:

John L. Lewis is our leader,
We shall not be moved,
John L. Lewis is our leader,
We shall not be moved.
Jus' like a tree dat's planted by de water,
We shall not be moved.

Mitch is our district president . . .

You can tell de henchmen . . .

Run an' tell de super'tendent . . .[13]

When "We Shall Not Be Moved" was sung in the civil rights movement, the emphasis on specific people was dropped and activists spoke in the first verse of their goal—freedom:

> We are fighting for our freedom
> We shall not be moved,
> We are fighting for our freedom,
> We shall not be moved,
> Just like a tree, planted by the water,
> We shall not be moved.[14]

A similar shift is evident in another labor song that was adapted for use in the civil rights movement, "Which Side Are You On?" where the 1940s "good workers" become the 1960s "freedom lovers."[15]

Some songs became freedom songs when the activists changed only one word in an older song. The early version of "Over My Head I See Freedom in the Air" was "Over My Head I See Trouble in the Air," and "Woke Up This Morning With My Mind on Freedom" had come from a religious song, "Woke Up This Morning With My Mind on Jesus."[16] These songs were simple ones in which the title lines were repeated many times and, with minimal changes, they were transformed from songs about the trials of blacks and about religious commitment to songs that were, unquestionably, about freedom.

Civil rights activists introduced the theme of freedom to many other old songs as well. The singers of early versions of "Keep Your Eyes on the Prize" made no references to freedom—their theme was religious salvation. In a version from 1917, the singer looked forward to a goal of reaching heaven:

> When I get to heaven I'm going to sit down,
> Wear a white robe and a starry crown.[17]

A variant from 1925, called "Keep Yore Hand Upon the Chariot," stressed salvation as well:

> For the preacher's comin' an' he preach so bold,
> For he preach salvation from out of his soul.
> Oh, keep yore hand upon the chariot,
> An' yore eyes upon the prize![18]

The better known and later version of the song, collected by folklorists John Lomax and Alan Lomax, is "Keep Your Hand on the Plow." This version, too, continued to be a religious song in its detailed retelling of the Biblical story of Paul and Silas in jail.[19]

By the time the song was sung in the civil rights movement, its tenor had been entirely changed—"Keep Your Eyes on the Prize" was a freedom song in the truest sense of the word. The "prize" in the 1925 song version had been salvation, while the "prize" in 1960, when Guy Carawan taught the song to student leaders in Nashville, was freedom:

> Paul and Silas begin to shout,
> The jail door opened and they walked out,
> Keep your eyes on the prize, hold on.
>
> Freedom's name is mighty sweet,
> Black and white are gonna meet.
> Keep your eyes on the prize, hold on.[20]

Freedom was highlighted in the civil rights songs to such an extent there can be little doubt the protestors saw all their acts and sacrifices motivated by that desire. The illustrations offered indicate that freedom filled the thoughts and directed the actions of the civil rights activists. The songs argued for single-minded purpose and devotion to one goal. They provided details about how freedom would be manifested in the lives of the activists and what activists must do to achieve their goal.

THE ACTIVISTS' SELF-DEFINITION: "WE ARE NOT AFRAID"

We can better understand the self-definition African American protestors created for themselves in their songs by analyzing a number of the verbal techniques they used. The freedom songs are full of personal references and self-allusions that provide information about the how the activists viewed themselves. This is worth noting, particularly because evidence suggests that self-reference did not always come easily to blacks in America. David Gates, in a review of the book of American slave narratives, *Bullwhip Days: The Slaves Remember*, made the observation that white attempts to rob slaves of their identities had been so successful that in "their" stories, "slaves tended to characterize their masters vividly, and themselves not at all."[21] The interviews with former slaves on which the book was based were conducted in the 1930s. In the years between 1930 and 1960, it appears that blacks had reclaimed their sense of self sufficiently to make many allusions to themselves and their place in the world. The civil rights songs advanced this rediscovery of self. The singers placed themselves as the subjects of many songs, with the individual or group initiating action and making things happen. A close look at the personal pronouns used in the songs is informative.

Individual and Collective Identity

The freedom songs, as they have been recorded, overwhelmingly feature self-references, with heavy use of such personal pronouns as "I," "we," "our," and "you," with the "you" clearly referring to a member of the singing group. In many songs, like "We Shall Overcome," "We Shall Not Be Moved," "Over My Head I See Freedom in the Air," and "I Love Everybody," virtually every line contains these references to self. The sheer frequency of self-references suggests that the activists were concerned with their own stories and with setting forth a clear identity for themselves. The songs provided a potent outlet for this emerging self-definition, one well-suited to the goals of the movement and easily shared.

By far the most prevalent pronouns were those of the first person, referring to an individual or group self. There are reasonable explanations for expecting either that the songs of the civil rights movement would primarily retain the individual emphasis of the earlier songs from which they had evolved *or* that they would be heavily weighted toward an emphasis on group unity and "we." On one hand, many of the civil rights songs were derived from older, traditional songs that had their roots in religious music. In those songs, the predominant pronouns referred to the first person singular, stressing the personal relationship between the individual and his or her God.

On the other hand, the communication strategies of any mass movement must serve to unify group members and encourage new converts. When activists for a cause use the pronouns "we," "us," and "our," they tacitly propose that a cohesive group already exists, and, in so doing, subtly circumvent a conscious decision on the part of the individual to join the group. Eric Hoffer wrote, in *The True Believer*, that in mass movements the communication is so focused on group unity that onlookers must expect the "surrender of the individual's will, judgment and advantage."[22] Such a surrender would result, it seems, in the eschewing of any strategy highlighting the individual will, as the use of references to "I" might.

What we find in the use of first person pronouns in the freedom songs is that neither of these influences, alone, prevailed. Although the first person was stressed, the focus shifted in what initially seemed a haphazard way, from "I" to "we." Some of the traditional songs that originally featured the first person singular were changed by activists to stress the group while others of the old songs were left unchanged. In certain songs, the pronoun use shifted between "I" and "we" from verse to verse or from verse to chorus.

Upon closer study, pronounced patterns of use become apparent and provide information regarding how the singers defined themselves. The patterns suggest that the songs were designed to both encourage a view of the self as autonomous and to unify individuals into a potent group. It is apparent that, generally, when the singers referred to feelings, faith, or commitment to the cause, they focused on the individual self and spoke of "I." Singers substituted the use of "we" when they described actions, past, present, or future. The singers sang of what "we" have done or will do, and, by so doing, built unity in terms of the actual undertakings of the group.

This split emphasis, with much concentration on the group, but with a marked persistence in singing of one's own personal involvement, brings to attention important functions of the songs in defining being. The patterns suggest an emphasis on the importance of the *individuals.* Although many social movements rely on the suppressing of individual will and judgment, the songs of the civil rights movement defined people as autonomous agents who chose to join their individual commitment and faith with others, in order to accomplish certain acts.

That so many average people stepped forward, with little history of organizing or speaking out for themselves, to take part in the civil rights movement suggests that these people were looking for autonomy and were willing to help themselves. The activists believed that they had to learn to do for themselves. Willie Peacock, a member of SNCC and worker for voter registration, argued that "Freedom doesn't come as a gift," a sentiment echoed by Gussie Nesbitt, a domestic worker who refused to ride the buses in Montgomery: "I wanted to be one of them that tried to make it better. I didn't want somebody else to make it better for me."[23] The activists believed that "You don't liberate people—you teach them how to liberate themselves,"[24] which made it important for them to communicate to people regarding their individual strength and power, as well as about the power of the group as a whole.

The activists gave special attention to individuals when they frequently remarked upon the specific people who began the singing, added new verses to songs, and encouraged others to sing. Activists told many stories, for instance, in which they stressed situations where songs were started by a lone voice or by a person who would not usually be thought of as a leader. Unlike some traditional attitudes toward communication that imply great men are the only catalysts of change, the activists suggested that the average person could be the starting place, by beginning alone but encouraging others to join in. The "indescribable" power of the song "We Shall Overcome" came, according to activists, from "a thousand voices singing as one," from "a half-dozen . . . behind the bars of the Hinds County prison," from "old women singing it on the way to work," and from "students singing it as they were being dragged away to jail."[25] Reagon remembered that one group of inspiring songleaders in the movement was made up of three elementary school children.[26] Julius Lester summarized the attitudes of many activists toward this attribute of song when he asserted that every person at the mass meetings was a "freedom singer," adding, "they don't need anyone to sing to them, because each of them has a song in his own soul."[27] In their references, the activists often spoke of the people who were engaged in the singing rather than simply reducing them to a faceless mass. Blacks had been deprived their identities by whites for countless years; they seemed unwilling to commit the same sin against one another.

In the songs, one pattern that reminded listeners of the role of the individual was the use of the pronoun "I" when the singers were referring to personal beliefs and thoughts that may have been shared by others but, necessarily, derived from the individual. The use of "I" was associated with verses stressing personal spiritual involvement in the movement, resulting in the implication that the group was capable of action only because it was composed of individuals with strong personal commitment. We can see this pattern in the song "Keep Your Eyes on the Prize."

The versions of "Keep Your Eyes on the Prize" that appeared in the traditional repertoire of black singers as early as 1917 stressed religious themes. The singer sang of personal goals associated with religious belief ("When I get to heaven I'm going to sit down/ Wear a white robe and a starry crown"); conversed as an individual with Satan ("Go away, Satan, let me be,/ You fooled my brother but you can't fool me"); or generally witnessed to others ("Keep your hand to the plough, hold on").[28] It was only in the song version popular during the civil rights movement that the overall focus of the song changed and the first person plural was included. In fact, in the civil rights version, the emphasis on the group was overwhelming, *but* the first person singular was retained in key places.

The use of "we" in "Keep Your Eyes on the Prize," during the civil rights movement, was reserved for the description of group actions in which blacks had been, and would continue to be, engaged. The singers referred to "the day we started to fight," and their plans that "we're gonna board that big Greyhound," and that "we're gonna ride for civil rights." When issues of feelings and beliefs arose, however, singers emphasized the individual, and his or her personal stand, by using the first person singular. The switch in pronouns is evident in such verses as:

> I know what I think is right,
> Freedom in the souls of black and white.

and

> Got my hand on the Gospel plow,
> I wouldn't take nothin' for my journey now.

When the issue was one of choice about becoming involved in the struggle, individuals spoke for themselves, saying "I wouldn't take nothin' for my journey now." The assertions of the individual voice were highlighted in the song because they were used sparingly.

"This Little Light of Mine" is another example of a song mixing the use of "I" and "we" along the lines of personal commitment and group action. The word "light" in the song was used as a metaphor both for love, a personal feeling derived from the individual, and for freedom, the goal of individuals, perhaps, but advanced by the actions of the group:

> The light that shines is the *light of love*,
> Lights the darkness from above . . .

and

> We've got the *light of freedom*,
> We're gonna let it shine . . .

In the song, the light/love usage was always associated with the individual by use of the first person singular. Singers claimed:

> The light that shines is the light of love . . .
> I'm gonna shine my light both far and near,
> I'm gonna shine my light both bright and clear.

Later in the song, the use of the "I" appeared again, as the singers claimed this light of love was a gift from God.

The singers associated the use of "I" with the individual's ability to love. In contrast, when they sang of the "light" as a metaphor for freedom, they associated it with the group and the pronoun "we." For instance, certain verses assert:

> We've got the light of freedom
> We're gonna let it shine,

and

> Deep down in the South
> We're gonna let it shine.

This association of "I" with love and "we" with freedom provides us with insight to verses of "This Little Light of Mine" in which the meaning is otherwise ambiguous. For instance, in the verse "All on Chief Pritchett, I'm gonna let it shine," it is not clear whether the reference to "it" was to love or freedom. But, since the pronoun "I" was matched with love in every other case, the appearance of "I" in this verse suggests that the interpretation should be that Pritchett was to be viewed as the recipient of love, not as an obstacle to freedom. Likewise, the use of "I" in the verse "All in the jailhouse, I'm gonna let it shine" suggested that, even in jail, the appropriate response was a loving one.

This pattern of pronoun use was evident in many other freedom songs. When freedom was sung of as a goal, it was generally described as "our" goal—"everybody says freedom." The singers asserted that:

> *We* are fighting for our freedom
> We shall not be moved . . .
>
> The truth will make *us* free . . .

and that:

> *We'll* find freedom on the other side.[29]

Implicit in this treatment was the argument made by many civil rights leaders, most notably Martin Luther King, Jr., that no person, black or white, could be truly free until all people shared freedom.[30]

The use of the first person singular in these songs repeatedly defined the individual as feeling and as highly committed to the cause, as well as to the higher ideals upon which the movement was based. Often, group action, so important to the progress of the movement, was described as dependent on this individual faith. In "This Little Light of Mine," the singers placed their references to "I" in ways that implied individuals were vitally important to the accomplishment of group goals. The pronoun "I" was used primarily in the first verse of the song, where it was likely to receive attention simply by virtue of being first, and in the two bridges, where it was emphasized because the bridges broke the rhythm and rhyme pattern that unified the verses of the song.[31] By using the pronoun "I," with its association with love, in these segments of the song, the singers implicitly stressed the individual and her or his ability to love as foundational to all else.

In "We Shall Overcome," activists stressed the pronoun "we" but retained the use of "I" in a telling way. Successful group action, the song suggested, was underpinned by strong individual commitment and belief. The lines describing action and transient states of mind, such as fear, contained the pronouns "we" and "us." These lines were grouped around another quite different one, however, that repeatedly reminded the singers and listeners of the personal source of strength. This line, "Deep in my heart, I do believe," celebrated the individual and his or her abiding faith, a faith sufficient to make action and overcoming possible. For "us" to overcome, each individual must be convinced of the inevitability of that goal, so the song continued to assert that "Deep in my heart, *I* do believe, we shall overcome someday." The proximity of the "we shall overcome" and the "I do believe" could lead the listener to perceive a connection between the two, with the goal of overcoming dependent on individual belief. The result was likely to be an implicit understanding of the role of the activist as one-in-many, an important component of the group, but never subsumed entirely into it.

The emphasis on the need for each individual to have a solid personal commitment was apparent in other freedom songs as well. To sing "And before we'll be slaves, we'll be buried in our graves" would have carried a very different meaning than did "Oh Freedom" as it was sung in the movement: "And before I'll be a slave, I'll be buried in my grave." The former presumes to let the group speak for the individual and makes a claim that one person cannot make for another. The willingness to die for a cause must come from deep inside a person, and no one can fairly make assumptions about the relative value another may place on life versus liberty. The song as sung in the movement depicted each person as taking symbolic responsibility for his own level of commitment, saying, in effect, "I, personally, would rather be dead than enslaved." The line had the force of a vow made, or a promise to oneself. By articulating these words, the singer was both communicating to him or herself about the extreme commitment felt for the cause and providing a kind of challenge to others who might then be inspired by the strength of conviction. When activists sang in the first person singular, they also emphasized the importance of each individual life, avoiding any trivialization of death by singing of many deaths in what could have been perceived as a cavalier tone.

The personal commitment suggested by the use of the first person singular was also apparent in the song "Ain't Gonna Let Nobody Turn Me 'Round." Although we might expect a group of marchers to sing "Ain't gonna let nobody turn *us* around," referring to the progress of the literal march, the song seemed to speak more to the personal commitment made and the personal intention to persevere. The danger, it seems, was not so much that the group could be turned back as that individuals would be discouraged by jail sentences and injunctions making their actions illegal. The abdication of individuals was the one thing that could really threaten the movement, and the song reinforced individual commitment, not the obvious commitment of the group persona.

The focus, in many of these songs, on the individual and his or her personal involvement also took the edge off any suggestion of mob action that might be inferred from the use of the first person plural in other songs. Instead of encouraging participants to give themselves over to the will of the group, the songs often subtly reminded activists that they were acting cooperatively with others but that the responsibility and commitment remained their own. This seemed to be the case, to some extent, in the song "Ain't Gonna Let Nobody Turn Me 'Round," as activists sang repeatedly of individual involvement. A similar interpretation was invited in the song "I'm On My Way." In this song, the singers referred to their own personal journeys toward "freedom land" while they also related their efforts to encourage others to embark on the journey as well:

> I'm on my way to freedom land,
> I'm on my way to freedom land,
> I'm on my way to freedom land,
> I'm on my way, great God, I'm on my way.
>
> I asked my brother to come with me,
> I asked my brother to come with me,
> I asked my brother to come with me,
> I'm on my way, great God, I'm on my way.
>
> If he can't go, I'm gonna go anyhow . . .
>
> If you can't go, don't hinder me . . .
>
> If you can't go, let your children go . . .

The singer here expressed personal intent and looked for the cooperation of others. The key, however, may be the determination with which the individual pledged to continue the journey, even if he or she must do so alone. The songs suggested that such unflagging individual commitment was the basis of all movement activity.

The songs repeatedly focused attention on the force of the individual, and her or his ability to make a difference. Activists stressed the responsibility of the individual to take part and simultaneously glorified the individual, arguing that each person who faced the costs of participating and chose, nonetheless, to lend support was a hero. When the songs repeatedly stressed, and drew individual singers to articulate, their faith and conviction, a definition of those individuals as essential elements of the synergy that was the civil rights movement evolved.

Although the use of the pronoun "I" ensured that protestors would always retain a sense of individuals and individual responsibility, it would be a mistake to overlook the power of the songs to bring people together. The most overwhelming image we have of the civil rights movement may be one of unity—people marching together, sitting in together, going to jail together, and, always, singing together. The songs that were such a visible part of movement activities did much to generate a strong sense of identification and unity among movement participants.

The words of the freedom songs themselves did much to create a sense of connectedness among movement participants, and let activists argue for unity and establish strong identification where they had previously been identified only by the facts of their lives. Although it is obviously not surprising that members of a protest movement must identify with one another and must work together, it is worthwhile to understand better how such identification is encouraged.

When the songs of the civil rights movement are compared with the earlier songs from which they were adapted, we can easily see that, while the earlier songs stressed the first person singular, the first person plural was more evident in the later songs. Although attention was certainly still given to the individual, the singers changed many songs in order to shift the focus to the group as a whole. In "Keep Your Eyes on the Prize," for instance, many new verses were added by civil rights singers in order to localize that song and adapt it to the specific conditions of the movement. In those verses, the word "we" appeared as many as eleven times, compared to only two or three references to "I." When "we" was used in such verses as:

> But the one thing that we did right,
> Was the day we started to fight

and

> We've met jail and violence too,
> But God's love has seen us through

the verses stressed the successes of the group and showed the result of acting together. Likewise, although "I'll Be All Right" was still popular in some places in the South, the activists of the civil rights movement almost always chose to sing its derivation, "We Shall Overcome."[32]

In "We Shall Overcome," the use of "we" in virtually every line of the song served as a constant, though perhaps subtle, assertion that this was not just a case of many people who happened to be singing together, but rather was a complex entity, the whole of which far exceeded the sum of the parts. The singers suggested that the capacity for action in the movement was largely contingent on the existence and maintenance of the "we." A pattern of apparent causality emerged, asserting that, *if* we stand "black and white together," *then* "we shall overcome." *If* "we'll walk hand in hand," *then* "we shall overcome." The group as group was placed at the center of all action depicted in the song.

In addition to the use of "we" to build unity, many of the songs contained references to other manifestations of unity. For example, in verses of "Keep Your Eyes on the Prize," like

> The only chain that a man can stand,
> Is that chain of hand in hand

and

> We're gonna ride for civil rights,
> We're gonna ride both black and white

the references to a chain made from clasped hands and to the joint actions of blacks and whites encouraged a sense of unity and togetherness. "(Everybody Says) Freedom" provides yet another example of the universal commitment to the movement goals, with activists going beyond personal pronouns of any type to assert that "*everybody* says freedom" and "*everybody* says civil rights."

"This Little Light of Mine" was also modified by the civil rights activists. These modifications, particularly the addition of new verses, allowed the singers to speak for group cohesion as well as for personal commitment. The song in its pre-civil rights form had represented an individual's promise to God, but activists transformed it into a song glorifying the ability of people to work together for a cause. The "little light" signified the "light of freedom" in parts of the civil rights version, and activists joined together to assert that "*we're* gonna let it shine." As noted, when they sang of love in "This Little Light of Mine," the activists used the first person singular, but they defined themselves as united in their commitment to their ultimate goal of freedom.

Another technique used to identify activists and define them as a "we" was the use of the words "you" and "I." With only a few exceptions, when singers referred in the song lyrics to the second person, their words were directed at a "you" within the group, as opposed to outsiders or adversaries. This usage did not serve to separate the singers from each other, except insofar as they were inherently separate as individuals. The references to "you" were almost always associated with "me" or "I," building the "we" that was so pervasive in the songs. Although the "light of love" in "This Little Light of Mine" was depicted as a gift from God to the individual, it was equally shared by others:

> The light that shines is the light of love,
> Lights the darkness from above,
> It shines on me and it shines on you,
> Shows what the power of love can do.

When the singers sang of experiences that must be expressed as personal, such as their thoughts or feelings, they often minimized the division between themselves and their fellows by encouraging the others to follow them in thought or belief. For instance, only the individual knows what occupied his or her thoughts upon waking and, so, the song must say:

> Woke up this morning with my mind
> (My mind it was) stayed on freedom.

The singers continued, however, by singing to one another in such a way as to encourage the sharing of a common goal. They sang:

> Ain't no harm to keep your mind stayed on freedom (3X)
> Hallelu, hallelu, hallelu, hallelu,
> Hallelujah![33]

and then followed with an interlude that urged:

> You got to walk walk
> You got to walk walk,
> You got to walk with your mind on freedom,

> You got to talk talk,
> You got to talk talk,
> You got to talk with your mind on freedom,
> Oh oh oh you got to walk walk, talk talk.

"Do What the Spirit Say Do" also combined the use of different personal pronouns, including in its verses "I," "we," and "you." In the shifting from singular to plural, and from first person to second person, the members of the singing group celebrated the complexity of their situation in which each person must be at his or her individual best in order to work together to form a group capable of action and change. The singers each stated their own intentions, singing:

> And what the spirit say do,
> I'm gonna do, Oh Lord . . .

while they appealed to others to follow their lead, singing:

> You gotta do what the spirit say do.

When the singers shifted from this personal statement of conviction and intent to the first person plural, "We're gonna do what the spirit say do," the implication was that what "we" can do was related to what "you and I" do, but different in a fundamental way. Here we might argue that the use of "we" synthesized the group as they spoke for all blacks.

In many of these songs, activists also issued an invitation to others to join them in their undertakings, thus, again, encouraging a working together and cohesiveness among individuals. For instance, in "If You Miss Me at the Back of the Bus," the singer addressed listeners, saying:

> If you miss me at the back of the bus,
> And you can't find me nowhere,
> Come on up to the front of the bus,
> I'll be ridin' up there.
> I'll be ridin' up there, I'll be ridin' up there.
> Come on up to the front of the bus, I'll be ridin' up there.
>
> If you miss me in the cotton field,
> And you can't find me nowhere,
> Come on down to the courthouse, I'll be voting right there.

The singer and listeners were identified in the song as compatriots, for otherwise one would not be missed by the others. In each verse, listeners were encouraged to make the move made by the singer, who had crossed the lines of segregation, and to join the singer.

In these many ways, the civil rights activists chose lyrics that promoted a strong sense of identification among participants in the movement. In each of these songs, whether the language choices stressed the unity of "we" or the individuality of "I" and "you," the participatory nature of the singing of the civil rights movement added an important unifying element to the songs. Even when the singers sang of "you" and "I" as distinct agents, they continued to sing with their coworkers, articulating their common goals and constituting a cohesive group. All singers would simultaneously be both "I" and "you," referring to themselves as "I" while the others referred to them as "you." The "you" was not a member of a separate group or an adversary but part of the "we" that was stressed in so many songs.

The choice of pronouns used in the many self-allusions in the freedom songs was an important factor in the sense of identity that activists encouraged in the freedom songs. By putting the people of the movement at the center of the songs, the singers defined themselves as the key to the change they sought. Although much emphasis was given to group unity and cohesiveness, the persistent appearance of the first person singular, used in reference to personal emotions and choices, always reminded the singers that the individual self was vitally important. The result of this combination was a definition of the self as autonomous but inevitably and thoroughly bound to others.

Definition of Self through Contrast

Beyond the consideration of personal pronouns in the songs, other patterns of self-allusion are evident, patterns that served to further define the activists. The references tend not to be direct ones stating "who we are"; instead, definition of self often came more obliquely, through contrasts to "what we are not."

Little in the civil rights songs offered an explicit definition of the nature of the people singing the songs. The songs did not assert, for instance, that "we are strong" or "I am proud" in the spirit of later Black Power claims that "black is beautiful" or "I'm black and I'm proud." In only one of the songs, "Which Side Are You On?", was there a direct descriptive phrase referring to the first person singular as a *being*. Here, the singer described himself as "a freedom son":

> My daddy was a freedom rider and I'm a freedom son . . .

Even in this song, with its direct claim to a certain identity, the relatively abstract term, "freedom son," was given concrete definition throughout the song not so much by the use of positive assertions as by contrast with the hated stereotype of the "uncle Tom." In the context of the song, a "freedom son" or "freedom lover" was everything that a "Tom" was not—committed to freedom, unafraid, and manly:

> My daddy was a freedom rider and I'm a freedom son,
> I'll stick right with this struggle until the battle's won.
>
> Don't Tom for Uncle Charlie, don't listen to his lies . . .
>
> You're either for the freedom rides or you Tom for Ross Barnett . . .
>
> Will you be an Uncle Tom or will you be a man . . .

This opposition between freedom lovers and Uncle Toms eliminated the middle ground of neutrality and asked listeners to choose to align themselves with one side or the other. The Uncle Tom was a stereotype, clearly defined in black culture and, as such, it lent clarity to the new definition juxtaposed to it.

Other negative assertions in the songs defined the nature of change that blacks sought from themselves. The existing definition of blacks, engineered by whites but, sadly, accepted by many blacks themselves, held that blacks would be passive and fearful in the face of white power. Singers sought to change that definition by warning listeners away from self-pity, saying "there'll be no more weepin' over me," and from doubt, saying "I love everybody. . . . The Klan can't make me doubt it."[34] In "We Shall Not Be Moved," "We'll Never Turn Back," and "Ain't Gonna Let Nobody Turn Me 'Round," singers continued to define themselves by describing what they would not do. By so doing, they argued for determination in the face of adversity and for an unwillingness to respond in the passive manner expected by whites.

Elsewhere, singers found still more ways to define themselves by detailing what they were not. In "We Shall Overcome," they sang "we are not alone" and "we are not afraid" and provided themselves with a point of view regarding their emotional responses to the realities of the movement. "We are not alone" reminded singers of the considerable number of people who supported the movement cause. Whether these reassuring words were sung by hundreds of people in a march or by a few in jail, the singers defined themselves as part of a group. James Farmer commented regarding the reassuring nature of this simple claim, when made jointly by activists. He described the incarceration of Freedom Riders, and remembered that two groups of activists, in separate rooms in the jail, joined to sing "We Shall Overcome." He said, that when "we finished the chorus, we stopped singing. And we felt good. . . . We had the boost we needed. We could face anything now. We were not alone."[35] This reminder of the unity and support of activists, attested to both by the words sung and by the very act of singing together, provided the members of the group with the affirmation they needed when feeling scared and vulnerable.

In the case of the line "we are not afraid," the singers faced explicitly the emotion that they could probably most expect to experience during their demonstrations and protests. Of course, fear was a very real part of each activist's life, and these lines implicitly suggest that there was good reason to be afraid—why else mention fear at all? The profession that they were not fearful would not likely convince anyone that there was no fear in the hearts of black activists. It did communicate an unwillingness to admit to the fear and to be cowed by it, however. Farmer spoke to this impulse, and detailed the meaning of the line "we are not afraid" for Freedom Riders in Jackson, Mississippi. As the Riders sang "We Shall Overcome,"

> the greatest fervor was reserved for the stanza "We are not afraid. We are not afraid. We are not afraid, today. Oh, deep in my heart, I do believe, we shall overcome, someday."
>
> I wished, I must confess, that singing it could make it so. It almost did. We sang loudly to silence our own fears. And to rouse our courage.[36]

The singing of the words did not negate the fear but, rather, seemed to give activists the sense that they could manage their fear. A white voter registration worker in Mississippi in the fateful summer of 1964 wrote to her family, and explained, in words similar to Farmer's, the function singing served for her:

> I tried consciously to overcome this fear. To relax, I began to breathe deep, think the words of a song . . . still the tension. . . .
> "We are not afraid. Oh Lord, deep in my heart, I do believe, We Shall Overcome Someday" and then I think I began to truly understand what the words meant. Anyone who comes down here and is not afraid I think must be crazy as well as dangerous to this project where security is quite important. But the type of fear that they mean when they, when we, sing "we are not afraid" is the type that immobilizes. . . . The songs help to dissipate the fear.[37]

To assert "we are not afraid" was to symbolically banish a key negative emotion that could weaken the movement.

Activists used their claim of the absence of fear to further reinforce their self-definition when they sang "I Ain't Scared of Your Jail." Sung to the tune of "The Old Gray Mare," "I Ain't Scared of Your Jail" seems to have been a song composed during the movement rather than deriving from traditional black music. The following description illustrates how powerful the song was in the activists' repertoire:

> The singers would use it like this: Rev. Fred Shuttlesworth would be lecturing everyone in the church, explaining all about nonresistance. "It's to be a silent demonstration," he would say. "No songs, no slogans, no replies to obscenities." Everyone would nod. "However," the reverend would add, "when you're arrested, sing your hearts out."
> So all the young people would file out of the church, solemn as deacons, quiet as mice. Then a cop would come along and shout, "You're all under arrest!" That was the cue. Suddenly there were five hundred bodies moving at once, their voice shouting out:
>
> > Ain't a-scared of your jail 'cause I want my freedom
> > I want my freedom . . .
> > I want my freedom . . .
> > I want my freedom . . .[38]

This unwillingness to give into fear, publicly avowed, defined the activists as a changed people, people who had taken custody of their emotions and actions.

Definition of Self as Spiritual

As might be expected, another aspect of the redefinition of blacks concerned the extent to which the activists embraced the heritage that had been earlier repudiated. Their new identity, as detailed by the freedom songs, was dependent on reviving a sense of pride in being black. This revival warrants close attention.

The call to emotionalism and spirituality that activists made when they argued for the centrality of their heritage in the civil rights movement was also evident in the words of freedom songs. In the songs, activists chose to retain the strong religious elements of the earlier songs from which the freedom songs were derived. The presence of these themes suggests more than just the survival of an old or outdated tradition. While the church continued to be important in the lives of many blacks, the nature of the movement went beyond specific religious orientations to achieve a more general spiritual appeal. With activists advocating nonviolence and agapic love in all aspects of the movement, the songs argued for a spirituality that transcended the religions many of them practiced.

The spiritual and religious themes of the civil rights songs were important in the definition of self in several ways. The extent to which references to God and religion were made suggests activists were emphasizing them for some purpose. Singers stressed the ways they were related to God and how their work was in concert with His will, while they avoided describing themselves as dependent on their religious beliefs or divine intervention in their lives. Religion was not a crutch for these activists—they defined themselves as autonomous, working alongside God to accomplish compatible goals. The spiritual themes in the freedom songs also enabled activists to address any lingering self-doubt about their worth and to counteract the white myth of their subhuman-ness.

The songs contained many allusions to "God" or "Lord." Several songs were addressed, ostensibly, to God, and God was referred to directly in many of the songs. Additionally, all but a very few of the songs were likely to have evoked thoughts of religion in listeners. A review of these songs indicates the extent to which activists retained elements of religion and spirituality in their lives.

In six of the songs under consideration here, "Ain't Gonna Let Nobody Turn Me 'Round," "Over My Head I See Freedom in the Air,"

"Do What the Spirit Say Do," "I'm On My Way," "Come By Here," and "Freedom Is a Constant Struggle," activists sang as if they were addressing their thoughts to God. They sang, for instance,

> Ain't gonna let nobody, Lordy, turn me 'round . . .

> Over my head, oh Lord, I see freedom in the air . . .

> I'm on my way, great God, I'm on my way . . .

> Oh Lord, we've struggled so long . . .

The words of these songs were meant, of course, for many ears. But, the manner of addressing God, as if in prayer, served as a reminder that faith was an important ingredient in the movement philosophy.

The religious overtones of "I'm On My Way" were reinforced because the song had originally been well-known to blacks as "I'm On My Way to Canaan Land" or the "heavenly land," with the change to "freedom land" occurring during the civil rights movement.[39] It seems likely that the earlier, more religious wording would be remembered and associated to some extent with the later songs, suggesting an ongoing religious undertone for movement activities. Similarly, the song sung in the movement as "(Everybody Says) Freedom" had been sung earlier as "(Everybody Says) Amen," a song with obvious religious connotations. "Woke Up This Morning With My Mind On Freedom" was derived from "Woke Up This Morning With My Mind on Jesus," a familiar church song in the South. "Oh Pritchett, Oh Kelley," too, had come to the movement from an older song titled "Rocking Jerusalem."[40]

Other songs retained a religious orientation because of the inclusion of stories that were recognizable from Christianity or because the songs had been popular church songs before they were adapted for the movement. "Keep Your Eyes on the Prize" began with the biblical story of Paul and Silas's miraculous escape from jail and made references to God, heaven, and "Jordan River." "Jacob's Ladder" referred to the biblical story, in Genesis 28, of Jacob's dream of a ladder to heaven. The activists, many of whom had been raised in the Christian churches of the South, would recognize the song and its connection with religion. This song was one sung often in the churches, as were "This Little Light of Mine" and "Michael Row the Boat Ashore." "We Shall Overcome," as well, had been adapted from a Baptist hymn, "I'll Be All

Right," that was still sung in its original form in some places in the South.[41]

Activists emphasized a religious tone in still other songs by the inclusion of the refrain "hallelujah," which brought with it the glorification of the Christian God. The word "hallelujah" appeared in all the verses of "I'm Gonna Sit at the Welcome Table," while the first verses also contained the biblical metaphors of the "welcome table" and the "streets of glory." "Woke Up This Morning With My Mind on Freedom" contained the refrain "hallelu, hallelu, hallelu, hallelu,/ hallelujah!" while in "Michael Row the Boat Ashore" singers sang of "Jordan River" and "Christian brothers," and finished every line with "alleluja." Activists rejoiced over their temporal accomplishments in spiritual terms in "Hallelujah, I'm A-Traveling" as well.

By retaining many religious references from the older songs, activists argued implicitly for the legitimacy of the civil rights undertaking and for the worth of the people engaged in the endeavor. The singers claimed that "God is on our side" and, in so doing, suggested that "our side" was unequivocally the morally correct side. Further, the singers asserted, in "Keep Your Eyes on the Prize," that "God's love will see us through" and verbally equated themselves with disciples Paul and Silas. Those men had been jailed, not because they were criminals, but because of religious beliefs and their commitment to a higher cause. By telling that story, activists suggested both that they were fighting for the same sort of higher cause and that, similarly, they were experiencing persecution because of their spiritual beliefs. These references were combined with others emphasizing a strong personal relationship between God and the singers.

Black religious beliefs are often noted for the ways that adherents define their relationship with God as very close and very personal. Folklorist Russell Ames commented on this characteristic in the antebellum slave songs, saying that "intimacy between man and God is extraordinarily pronounced in Negro spirituals compared with other folk songs."[42] Other researchers have indicated that black churchgoers continue to address God directly as one would treat a friend, in tones different from the reverence and distance evident in many white people's prayers. The perceived closeness to God persisted in the songs of civil rights and was suggested in such lyrics as "I'm going to tell God how you treated me." Here, in the one of the few references to "you" as an adversary found in these songs, the singer in "I'm Gonna

Sit at the Welcome Table" warned outsiders that their actions would not go unnoticed.

Activists stressed a special relationship with God in the songs that were ostensibly addressed to Him, including "Ain't Gonna Let Nobody Turn Me 'Round" and "Over My Head I See Freedom in the Air." In yet other songs, the singers' relationship with God was described as a familial one. Protestors identified themselves as "God's children" and, in "Oh Freedom," a similar tie was suggested when singers voiced their intention to "go *home* to my Lord and be free." By associating themselves and their goals with religious themes, the activists argued for a certain kind of self-definition. They described themselves as worthy of the support of God, and strong in their commitment that what they were doing was consistent with the goals of their religion.

Many of the songs of the civil rights movement stressed how blacks translated their spiritual beliefs in their daily lives. This was contrasted, then, with the ways that whites seemed to repudiate their avowed beliefs in their treatment of blacks. God, for the civil rights activists, was, of course, the same Christian God of whites, but blacks described a qualitatively different kind of relationship with God and enacted their religious beliefs in ways seemingly unknown to southern white Christians. In their descriptions of their beliefs, black activists were, in effect, suggesting they could beat white Christians at their own game.

Whites had introduced black slaves to Christianity *and* had introduced them to religious hypocrisy. While antebellum whites advocated the Christian way to their slaves, they gave them a modified and tainted form of Christianity, one that suited their purposes as slave owners. The testimony of former slaves indicated they were aware of the hypocrisy then, and it is clear the civil rights activists were aware of continued hypocrisy among whites who espoused certain beliefs in their churches on Sunday and yet could bomb black churches later on the same day.

The shared religion of blacks and whites, and the blacks' way of upholding it, served as a challenge and a rebuke to those whites who were Christians in name only. By contrasting themselves to whites in this area where traditions overlapped, blacks had a clear example of their superiority to hypocritical whites. In "Oh Pritchett, Oh Kelley," the activists were characterized as "God's children" who were held in jail by the men who became archetypes of southern racism, Laurie Pritchett and Asa Kelley. While the black Christians cried for mercy and prayed in jail, the white so-called Christians increased their bail.

In "I'm Gonna Sit at the Welcome Table," the singers contrasted the Christian welcome they would receive in God's heaven with their temporal situation. In heaven, they were assured of sitting at the "welcome table." On earth, their more immediate desire was to "sit at Woolworth's lunch counter." The irony was that people worthy of God's welcome had not received the welcome of their fellow humans in a lowly five and dime store. Zinn reported on Stokely Carmichael's singing of a verse of this song, "I'm gonna tell God how you treated me," during his imprisonment at Parchman Penitentiary during the Freedom Rides.[43] Such irony was implicit in all of the songs describing the comfort and aid blacks received from their God as opposed to the trials and degradation they faced from other humans.

The singers also highlighted the nonviolent philosophy of the movement and provided details illustrating how the philosophy was enacted. Very often in the songs, for instance, references to the violence of whites were juxtaposed with references to nonviolent responses by blacks. This contrast of two opposing types of behavior highlighted the difference between white and black attitudes and actions. In "Keep Your Eyes On the Prize," one verse explained that

> We've met jail and violence too
> But God's love has seen us through.

The spiritual references to God and to love offered a useful foil to the concrete reference to "jail" and the more general term, "violence." The use of the word "violence" here, although not clearly defined, was likely evocative of certain images for listeners. Because movement participants had met much violence, they would have no trouble imagining the concrete manifestations of the word. Any audience for the songs beyond the movement members would likely have a clear idea about specific acts of violence as well. The civil rights movement was carried into American homes by television and, because that medium is drawn to the dramatic and confrontational, many Americans had images of fire hoses and police dogs indelibly imprinted on their minds' eyes. Even such a fleeting reference to "jail and violence" as the one in "Keep Your Eyes On the Prize" was a potent reminder to listeners of what they had experienced, personally or vicariously.

Only such shared images of the civil rights movement gave concrete meaning to the following in "Keep Your Eyes On the Prize":

We're gonna board that big Greyhound,
Carryin' love from town to town.

For members of the movement and for Americans who followed the news, the Freedom Rides into the Deep South gave resonance to the line "We're gonna board that big Greyhound." The Greyhound buses ridden by blacks and whites to test the interstate desegregation rulings were attacked by white mobs, Riders were beaten, and buses were set ablaze. Photos of these Rides reached all corners of the United States, and alerted Americans to the ill treatment of people who were seeking to carry "love from town to town." These words dramatized the contrast of violence and nonviolence.

In other examples of the contrast between the violence of whites and the nonviolent response of blacks, activists stressed their ability to love those who hated them. Singers argued that they would continue to let the lights of freedom and love shine "all on Chief Pritchett," "all in the jail house," and "every time I'm bleeding." The agapic love of the civil rights movement was a recurrent theme in the songs, suggesting the singers used the songs both to define themselves as people capable of selfless, universal love and to provide them with strength to live up to that self-definition.

An apparently insignificant choice of personal pronouns in one song advanced this theme and emphasized the necessity of loving one's enemies. In the bridge of "This Little Light of Mine," singers related a conversation with God and of gifts received from Him. The narrative was cast in the first person singular, implying that the conversation was between God and the individual, with the first line saying, "On Monday he gave me the gift of love." There are many types of love, and the wording of the song seems to distinguish among them. If the words had been "On Monday, he gave *us* the gift of love," the meaning would have been slightly different, suggesting the love of each person singing for the others in his group ("we love each other"). As sung, the words suggested that the gift was a love for all others, not just for all of "us." When many voices joined, singing "He gave me the gift of love," the message became "you, and you, and you, and I each love" not "we love each other." All-inclusive, the song did not delineate between an in-group that was worthy of love and outsiders who were unlovable, but advertised the ability of the singer to love indiscriminately.

The lyrics of the freedom songs offered a definition of self that transcended typical human reactions to hostile treatment and established a sense of being more spiritual and selfless than most people, certainly than the southern bigots who were the primary adversaries of the civil rights movement, could achieve. How better to contradict and disprove a lingering definition of subhumanness than by demonstrating a degree of love and acceptance associated with Jesus Christ, Mahatma Gandhi, and others who are recognized as transcending the typical capabilities of men and women?

When activists sang about a close relationship with God and implied they merited divine support, they suggested that the goals of the movement were inevitably going to be reached. They did not, however, indicate that they believed they would achieve their goals simply as a result of divine intervention. God was represented as an interested and caring figure, who provided inspiration and spiritual support but was not directly responsible for day to day triumphs and failures. Rather, activists used their songs to represent themselves as autonomous agents who would draw on religious conviction to accomplish their own goals. The singers asserted their intentions to strive and work for themselves by relying on the love and strength that many saw as a gift from God. In their songs, black protestors challenged *themselves* to make changes that would, subsequently, bring about change in the conditions of the South. Their songs did not constitute a plea for help in changing the structure of the society but, rather, a declaration of their intent to make the changes necessary in their lives.

This emphasis on the individual's responsibility in bettering his or her own life was evident in many of the songs for civil rights. The relationship between God and the singers was stressed, but God was not portrayed as actively involved in the struggle of the activists. The singers themselves undertook the actions necessary to change their lives. In "Oh Pritchett, Oh, Kelley," the song in which the protestors were depicted as "God's children," it was still the mortal singer who addressed Pritchett and Kelley and urged them to release their prisoners. The words of "I'm Gonna Sit at the Welcome Table" also stressed the close relationship between the activists and God by the inclusion of the line, "I'm gonna tell God how you treated me." The singers continued to plan for accomplishing their own goals, however, singing "*I'm* gonna get my civil rights."

A close look at "Keep Your Eyes on the Prize" provides a better appreciation of the consistency of the black attitude toward their relationship with God. The song changed in crucial ways over 50 years.[44] In versions from the early 1900s, religion was the central theme; later versions, including the civil rights variant, contained fewer references to religion, suggesting the theme, in general, was becoming less important to the people who sang the song. The conception of God's relationship with the singers, however, remained consistent from the early religious versions to the later, more secular ones. The singers, in 1917 and 1963, argued for their autonomy and for a cooperative effort between God and people.

In all of the versions of "Keep Your Eyes on the Prize," the singers referred to God and His power but emphasized what people could do to change their own lives. The song, as collected by Cecil Sharp in 1917, suggested a God of some power, involved in the running of the world.[45] The end of the world and the nature of heaven were religious themes that clearly implied a God, and one direct reference was made to divine intervention. The intervention was not so much *for* the singer, however, as it was *against* the unnamed hypocrite to whom the verse was addressed:

Some of these mornings at the rising sun
O God's going to stop your lying tongue.

As far as the singers' progress was concerned, it seemed to fall much more clearly into their own hands:

I'm going to heaven and I hain't going to stop,
There hain't going to be no stumbling-block.

The singers also addressed Satan personally, not asking God to protect them but, rather, taking responsibility for such matters and warning:

Go away, Satan, let me be,
You fooled my brother but you can't fool me.

In addition to the personal orientation evident in these verses, the choruses of all the variants encouraged a similar perseverance and single-mindedness, whether they urged auditors to "Keep your hand on the plow, hold on" or "Keep your eyes on the prize, hold on."

Later variants of "Keep Your Eyes on the Prize" were also explicitly religious but referred to God only implicitly. Early versions often began with the words "Paul and Silas, bound in jail," and referred to the biblical story that ended with the escape of these two men.[46] The lines

> Paul and Silas begin to shout,
> The jail door opened and they walked out

might *suggest* God's hand in the escape, because they were based on a biblical passage and because, in black parlance, to "shout" is often associated with religious worship. According to folklorists John A. Lomax and Alan Lomax, a "shout" included elements of song and dance, all focused on the praising of God.[47] This word choice, although it could have been interpreted more generally to mean to yell or call loudly, was likely to have evoked thoughts associated specifically with Paul and Silas's praising of God. In the songs, God's role in Paul and Silas's escape was not mentioned in any more explicit way. The jail doors opened, according to the song, in response to the acts, the songs, of the men who called upon their faith. Paul and Silas become the central actors, responsible for their own freedom.

The version of the song as it reached the civil rights movement had a much more secular tone than the earlier ones, with many topical verses describing situations the activists had experienced. Here, the singers referred to God's love and its importance to them, but made no mention of reliance on God or religion. The singers put the striving of humans at the center of progress in the movement. Paul and Silas were still described as "shouting" and this act was represented as necessary to the opening of the jail doors. The activists, themselves, were depicted as involved and autonomous, with many lines telling what "we're gonna do . . ." to advance the cause. The singers claimed a personal understanding of right and wrong and suggested that this knowledge had motivated their actions.

The activists, in their emphasis on their own power to change their lives, did not repudiate God but, rather, sang of the gifts they received from God, gifts enabling them to live the lives they desired and to respond in positive ways to their opposition. This is especially clear in "This Little Light of Mine." In the second bridge of the song, singers enumerated God's gifts to them and, with the last line, designated the end to which these gifts should be used:

> On Monday he gave me the gift of love
> Tuesday peace came from above
> Wednesday he told me to have more faith
> Thursday he gave me a little more grace
> Friday he told me to watch and pray
> Saturday he told me just what to say
> Sunday he gave me the power divine
> To let my little light shine.

For traditional Christians, this song may have been reminiscent of the parable of the talents. In this well-known Bible story, three servants were given money by their master. The two servants who used the gift to make more money were praised and their master gave them increased rank and power. The sole servant who, out of fear and perhaps laziness, hid the gift away and failed to build on it, was reviled. The gifts from God outlined in "This Little Light of Mine," likewise, were to be used in order to build and improve the lives of the recipients. To fail to make positive use of a gift from God was to fail God.

In all of these instances, the civil rights activists chose to present a view of the world in which religion and God played an important role but only in providing them with the raw material necessary to improve their own lot. For those who sang the songs, the religious or godly was manifested through the acts of women and men. The assertion that God was on the side of civil rights suggested a legitimacy to the actions of activists, but the singers placed the acts of mortals at the center of attention. Bernice Reagon commented on this tendency among singers to focus on their own roles in effecting change, in words that demonstrated the level of strategizing that often went into decisions about the language used in the songs:

> In "We Shall Overcome" there's a verse that says "God is on our side," and there was a theological discussion that said maybe we should say, "We are on God's side." God was lucky to have us in Albany doing what we were doing. I mean what better case would He have? So it was really like God would be very, very happy to be on my side. There's a bit of arrogance about that, but that was the way it felt.[48]

The "bit of arrogance" indulged in by activists can be interpreted as an indication of the progress they had made in redefining themselves. They were not willing to hide behind their religion or to placate themselves with promises of heavenly reward or divine intervention. So morally correct was their goal, that they did not question their ability to achieve it.

SUMMARY

By attending to the ways that the activists referred to themselves, we learn who those people believed themselves to be and who they aspired to be. The singers clearly identified freedom as the goal that motivated them above all others and focused their songs on defining themselves as people who could achieve that goal. Their definition was carefully crafted to encourage a balanced view of the self as autonomous yet vitally linked to others. The civil rights activists were seldom direct in making descriptive claims about themselves. Instead, they described themselves by saying what they were *not* and by identifying spirituality as a essential component of their makeup. By so doing, the activists avoided a boasting or self-aggrandizing tone that might have been unproductive in terms of attracting new participants to the movement.

In the songs of the civil rights movement, the singers argued for a sense of being radically opposed to the being that whites would perpetuate for blacks. Important in their songs of self-definition were themes of individuality, of autonomy, and of a transcendent discipline and spirituality. They described themselves as people undergoing changes, in the process of becoming stronger and more loving.

In addition to studying the freedom songs to understand how activists defined themselves, we can see in the songs a view of the world as it was perceived and recreated by the singers of the freedom songs. This must be so, for any self-definition implies the interacting of the self with other people and with the context in which people find themselves.

NOTES

1. Pete Seeger and Bob Reiser, *Everybody Says Freedom* (New York: W.W. Norton, 1989), 17.

2. Joe Azbell in Juan Williams, *Eyes on the Prize: America's Civil Rights Years, 1954-1965* (New York: Viking, 1987), 74.

3. Ida Holland in Kay Mills, *This Little Light of Mine: The Life of Fannie Lou Hamer* (New York: Dutton, 1993), 64.

4. From "Ain't Gonna Let Nobody Turn Me Round" in Guy Carawan and Candie Carawan, *We Shall Overcome!: Songs of the Southern Freedom Movement* (New York: Oak, 1963), 60-61. See also Seeger and Reiser, *Everybody Says,* 74-75. All references to song texts are drawn from these two sources, except where otherwise noted. The texts of the songs and bibliographic information appear in an appendix.

5. From "I'm On My Way."

6. From "Keep Your Eyes on the Prize."

7. From "Come By Here" and "Freedom Is a Constant Struggle."

8. These comments are based on the songs as they appear in the appendix. It should be noted that the songs were often changed spontaneously during marches and other activities, where activists extemporized and added verses or lines based on their current situation. The verses recorded here seem to have been the core of the songs.

9. Kenneth Burke, *Philosophy of Literary Form,* 3d ed., rev. (Berkeley: University of California Press, 1973), 70.

10. Carroll C. Arnold, *Criticism of Oral Rhetoric* (Columbus: Merrill, 1974), 120.

11. "I'll Be All Right" in Guy Carawan and Candie Carawan, *Freedom Is a Constant Struggle: Songs of the Freedom Movement* (New York: Oak, 1968), 138-139. Early versions of "Oh, Freedom" in William E. Barton, "Hymns of the Slave and Freedman, *New England Magazine* (January 1899), 98; Nathaniel Dett, *Religious Folk Songs of the Negro* (Hampton, VA: Hampton Institute Press, 1927), 110; Waldemar Hille, *The People's Song Book* (1948. New York: Oak, 1961), 21.

12. Bruce Jackson, "The Glory Songs of the Lord," in *Our Living Traditions: An Introduction to American Folklore,* ed. Tristram Potter Coffin (New York: Basic, 1968), 117.

13. George Korson, *Coal Dust on the Fiddle* (Hatboro, PA: Folklore Associates, 1965), 315.

14. Carawan and Carawan, *We Shall Overcome,* 21.

15. Hille, *People's Song Book*, 92.

16. The switch in words from "over my head I see trouble in the air" to "over my head I see freedom in the air" is documented by Bernice Reagon, the singer who introduced the change, in Bernice Johnson Reagon, "Songs of the Civil Rights Movement 1955-1965: A Study in Culture History" (Ph.D. diss., Howard University, Washington, D.C., 1975), 134-135. References to the word change from "woke up this morning with my mind on Jesus" to "woke up this morning with my mind on freedom" are found in Carawan and Carawan, *We Shall Overcome*, 81, and Josh Dunson, *Freedom in the Air: Song Movements of the Sixties* (New York: International, 1965), 65.

17. Cecil Sharp, *English Folk Songs from the Southern Appalachians*, volume 2 (London: Oxford University Press, 1932), 292.

18. Dorothy Scarborough, *On the Trail of Negro Folk-Songs* (Cambridge: Harvard University Press, 1925), 256.

19. See "Keep Yo' Hand on the Gospel Plow" in Newman I. White, *American Negro Folk-Songs* (Cambridge: Harvard University Press, 1928), 115, and "Keep Your Hand on the Plow" in John A. Lomax and Alan Lomax, *Folk Song, U.S.A.*, (New York: New American Library, 1975), 468-469.

20. It is interesting that civil rights activists believed they had created the reference to "the prize" when, in fact, the reference came, at least, from the 1925 version. In Carawan and Carawan, *We Shall Overcome*, 111, the authors attribute the word change to activist Alice Wine in 1956.

21. David Gates, "Our Stories, Our Selves," *Newsweek*, 23 January 1989, 64.

22. Eric Hoffer, *The True Believer* (New York: Harper, 1966), 36.

23. Willie Peacock in Seeger and Reiser, *Everybody Says*, 166; Gussie Nesbitt in Henry Hampton and Steve Fayer, *Voices of Freedom: An Oral History of the Civil Rights Movement from the 1950s through the 1980s* (New York: Bantam, 1990), 25-26.

24. Willie Peacock in Seeger and Reiser, *Everybody Says*, 181.

25. Wyatt Tee Walker in Carawan and Carawan, *We Shall Overcome*, 11.

26. Reagon, "Songs of the Civil Rights Movement," 96.

27. Julius Lester, "Freedom Songs in the South," *Broadside* 39 (Feb. 7, 1964), 1.

28. Sharp, *English Folk Songs*, 292.

29. From "We Shall Not Be Moved," "We Shall Overcome," and "Keep Your Eyes on the Prize."

30. Occasionally, the singers sang of their *thoughts* about freedom. In such songs as "Woke Up This Morning With My Mind on Freedom" and "Oh Freedom," the very personal nature of the claims necessitated the use of the first person singular.

31. A bridge in a song is a transitional element that separates but links sections of the song. The bridges of "This Little Light of Mine" are noted in the appendix.

32. Reagon, "Songs of the Civil Rights Movement," 132.

33. From "Woke Up This Morning With My Mind on Freedom."

34. From "Oh Freedom" and "I Love Everybody."

35. James Farmer, *Lay Bare the Heart: An Autobiography of the Civil Rights Movement* (New York: Arbor House, 1985), 8.

36. Farmer, *Lay Bare the Heart,* 6-7.

37. Elizabeth Sutherland, ed. *Letters from Mississippi* (New York: McGraw-Hill, 1965), 150-151.

38. Seeger and Reiser attribute this story to Len Holt, *Everybody Says,* 112. Pete Seeger tells the story, in almost the exact words, on "We Shall Overcome: The Complete Carnegie Hall Concert," Columbia C2K 45312, re-release, 1989.

39. White, *American Negro Folk-Songs,* 118; Seeger and Reiser, *Everybody Says,* 56.

40. Daniel J. Gonczy, "The Folk Music Movement of the 1960s: Its Rise and Fall," *Popular Music and Society* 10.1 (1985): 24.

41. Reagon, "Songs of the Civil Rights Movement," 132.

42. Russell Ames, *The Story of American Folk Song* (New York: Grosset, 1955), 133.

43. Howard Zinn, *SNCC: The New Abolitionists,* 2nd ed. (Boston: Beacon, 1965), 57.

44. Sharp, *English Folk Songs,* 292; Scarborough, *Trail of Negro Folk-Songs,* 256; White, *Negro Folk-Songs,* 115; Lomax and Lomax, *Folk Song, U.S.A.,* 468-469.

45. Sharp, *English Folk Songs,* 292.

46. Lomax and Lomax, *Folk Song, U.S.A.,* 468-469.

47. Lomax and Lomax, *Folk Song, U.S.A.,* 219.

48. Bernice Reagon in Hampton and Fayer, *Voices of Freedom,* 107-108.

IV

"I See Freedom in the Air": Defining a View of the World

With the singing of their freedom songs, civil rights activists responded to the limiting definition under which they had struggled and began to craft a new definition for African Americans. As they did so, there also emerged a view of the world. The worldview offered in the freedom songs was consistent with the self-definition crafted by the singers. In exploring this formulation of a worldview, we can better understand the ways the singers conceived of the world and its influence on the activists themselves, on other people who populated their world, and on the interactions between activists and others.

A WORLD OF IDEALISM AND PRAGMATISM

The activists of the civil rights movement described their world with a masterful mix of idealism and pragmatism. They balanced abstract references with very specific descriptions to create a view of the world that was both inspiring and compelling to activists. In this world, abstract ideals were revered but were also necessarily translated into concrete reality. The strong spiritual core of the movement was evident in the songs but the songs also served to clearly define, in more specific terms, the kinds of practical change necessary for the movement to progress.

This rhetorical balance was argued for in the activists' descriptions of their central goal of freedom and the ways to achieve it. They spoke of the specific joys and hardships of movement life while maintaining a sense of larger purpose. By tapping into the most general shared values and the most specific shared experiences of the protestors, singers imbued the songs with enormous potential to bring about change in their thinking and behavior. The balance they struck in their songs seems to have provided civil rights activists with the inspiration to move forward, in the face of great opposition, while they remained realistic about the nature of the opposition.

The shift in the songs from abstract ideal to concrete manifestation was most evident in the progression of verses in the songs. The verses sung first in the songs were usually verses that had been retained from older, traditional religious songs. As the activists for civil rights adopted the old songs, they introduced changes, tailoring the messages to their needs. In making changes, however, they also preserved much of the original sense of the songs and, in many cases, the similarities between the old songs and the new are as informative as are the differences.

The verses from the old songs typically stressed universal, abstract issues and were left untouched when sung in the civil rights movement, presumably, because their appeal transcended the specifics of different situations and occasions to speak to the larger concerns of the disfranchised. The issues of civil rights were fundamentally the same issues that had been important in black lives for many years, and these became the subjects of the first verses of the freedom songs. The verses that followed these first verses were more likely to be of the activists' making, verses localizing the broader issues to the day-to-day struggles for civil rights.

A closer look at the first verses of the freedom songs demonstrates how these key verses indexed the material that came after them, which provided information about how the verses should be interpreted. In their universal treatment of ideas, the singers dealt in relatively abstract and ambiguous terms that could be applied to a variety of different situations and would provide points of easy identification for almost any listener. For instance, "Oh, Freedom" can be traced back to the years following the Civil War, through Reconstruction and the labor movement, to its revival again during the civil rights movement. In all versions of the song, the first verses remained nearly identical. A version collected in the 1920s,

> Oh, freedom! Oh, freedom!
> Oh, freedom over me!
> An' befo' I'd be a slave,
> I'll be buried in my grave,
> An' go home to my Lord an' be free,[1]

differs in only incidental ways from the version commonly sung during the civil rights movement:

> Oh Freedom Oh Freedom
> Oh Freedom over me over me,
> And before I'll be a slave
> I'll be buried in my grave,
> And go home to my Lord and be free.

This verse, the rhetorical core of the song, suited the needs of recently emancipated slave, labor unionist, and civil rights marcher alike because the language was general enough to express the feelings of any persecuted people, stressing the concerns and desires of the oppressed. The verses that followed addressed the more specific concerns of each group of activists.

This pattern was evident in other songs as well. The first verse of "Come By Here" asked only for the Lord's presence:

> Come by here, my Lordy, come by here.

The later verses provided the civil rights-oriented reasons for the request:

> Churches are burning here, come by here . . .

> Someone's shooting, Lord, come by here. . . .

Similarly, "I Love Everybody" began with that claim, "I love everybody," and the following verses added localized details like "The Klan can't make me doubt it." Rather than begin "Keep Your Eyes on the Prize" with the specific details of their own trials and strivings, civil rights activists retained the first verses from earlier versions, verses telling the story of Paul and Silas. This was a narrative about specific people, yes, but its use in this song seemed to take on archetypal meaning for singers, with Paul and Silas standing for all the individuals who had been jailed because of their involvement in a moral struggle.

In other songs, the chorus of the song, repeated after every verse, or certain lines that appeared in every verse, accomplished a similar purpose. While the verses of "Hallelujah, I'm A-Traveling" detailed the specific victories of the Montgomery bus boycott, the sit-ins, and the Freedom Rides, the singers always came back to the chorus:

> Hallelujah, I'm a-traveling,
> Hallelujah, ain't it fine,
> Hallelujah, I'm a-traveling,
> Down freedom's main line . . .

which returned attention to the larger goal of the movement. In "We'll Never Turn Back," the verses told of time spent in jail and of the murder of activist Herbert Lee, but the chorus was, again, always more general, more abstract:

> But we'll never turn back,
> No we'll never turn back,
> Until we've all been free and we have equality.

The form of the songs suggested that, in the continuing story of civil rights campaigns, the specific details might change but the ultimate goal remained the same, as it had been for all protestors who had voiced these words.

In their relative abstraction, the first verses and choruses of the freedom songs did more to set an inspirational tone or mood than to provide specifics about worldview or actions to be taken. These verses were more likely to retain strong biblical or spiritual imagery and, therefore, they framed the verses following them in that spiritual light, and invited listeners to respond to the entire songs as spiritual songs. When later verses of some songs spoke of the "fight" or "struggle" for freedom or of going to jail, those words were softened by virtue of their context. The prevailing tone was one of spirituality so references to more agonistic interaction were likely to be understood in those terms.

The verses following the opening ones in the freedom songs were often very different from those first verses. Where the first verses universalized meaning, conveying ideas on a relatively high level of abstraction and spirituality, the later verses localized meaning and tied ideas to the specifics of the civil rights movement and, often, to certain campaigns in that movement.

We can find this universalization/localization pattern in most of the freedom songs. In the most famous of the songs, the first verse asserted:

> We shall overcome,
> We shall overcome,
> Deep in my heart, I do believe
> We shall overcome someday.

In following verses of the song, small changes provided the details of how the overcoming would be accomplished and the benefits that made the outcome worth striving for:

> We'll walk hand in hand . . .

> We'll all go to jail . . .

> We shall brothers be . . .

The details of the verses all seemed to be related to the first and most important verse while providing the kinds of details to which activists could more easily relate.

Many of the songs contained localizing verses that tailored songs to the different campaigns in which the activists were involved. In "I'm Gonna Sit At the Welcome Table," after the early, more general verses, the singers translated those verses into temporal terms closely related to the experiences of the activists. "I'm gonna sit at the welcome table" was given concrete meaning when they substituted "Woolworth's lunch counter" for "welcome table" in one of the verses. A verse that once may have encouraged religious audiences to aspire to heavenly reward, "I'm gonna walk the streets of glory," took on new meaning when activists walked the streets of Albany, Georgia, singing "I'm gonna get my civil rights." In the same way, as the chorus of "Hallelujah, I'm A-Traveling" spoke, in a general way, of the "traveling" of activists "down freedom's main line," the verses gave activists the opportunity to celebrate the successful stops they made along the way:

> I'm paying my fare on the Greyhound bus line,
> I'm riding the front seat to Montgomery this time.

> In Nashville, Tennessee, I can order a coke,
> The waitress at Woolworth's knows it's no joke.

> I walked in Montgomery, I sat in Tennessee,
> And now I'm riding for equality.

Activists included this combination of transcendental and pragmatic themes in most of the freedom songs and the technique seems to have been a conscious strategy. Pete Seeger and Bob Reiser remembered that:

> It became common to start with the name of the city or state one was singing in at the time, and then broaden the geographical area, or shrink it to become ever more specific. Thus a series of verses might be:
>
> > All over the state of Georgia . . .
> >
> > All over the southland . . .
> >
> > All over America . . .
> >
> > All over the world now . . .
>
> Or it could be:
>
> > All over the state of Georgia . . .
> >
> > All over the city of Atlanta . . .
> >
> > On this street called Peachtree . . .
> >
> > Here in this building . . .
> >
> > Deep in my heart . . .[2]

The technique enabled activists to argue continually, in their songs, both for their individual importance in the movement and the movement's place in the larger scheme of things.

The songs provided inspiration on an elevated level while giving details about the desired ends of protest and the means of achieving those ends. To accomplish movement goals, activists were urged to "love" and to "pray when the spirit say pray," but also to "picket" and to "vote when the spirit say vote."[3] The verses in "Oh Freedom" asserted that "there'll be no segregation over me" and then went on to provide details of what a world without segregation would entail:

> There'll be no more shooting over me . . .

There'll be no burning churches over me . . .

There'll be no more jail houses over me . . .

There'll be no more Jim Crow over me . . .

There'll be no more Barnett over me . . .

These verses detailed the specific burdens of segregation but the verses were joined together by a refrain that contained the emotional core of the song, where singers asserted their commitment to the end of segregation:

And before I'll be a slave,
I'll be buried in my grave,
And go home to my Lord and be free.

The song form chosen by activists provided them with the opportunity to strike an emotional chord on an abstract, universal level and to provide concrete points of reference for the emotion and inspiration as well.

Many of the freedom songs were structured in such a way that the first verse, the one that contained the most universal statements and constituted an emotional core for the song, was repeated as the final verse as well. The progression from general to specific, back to a restatement of the general again, resulted in a slightly different, amplified meaning at the end of these songs. Such amplification of meaning is evident in "Ain't Gonna Let Nobody Turn Me 'Round." The broadest statement referred to the activists' unwillingness to be swayed from their course of action or discouraged, and appeared in the first verse of the song—"I ain't gonna let nobody turn me 'round." Although that might seem to be the final word on the subject, with no need for embellishment, the verses enumerated the people and other obstacles capable of slowing the progress of the movement. These verses kept the song current because new details could be, and were, added easily. The additions chronicled a mounting number of obstacles for the activists that they had matched with a corresponding number of victories. Activists repeatedly faced situations, such as jailhouses and injunctions, and people, such as Albany Police Chief Pritchett and Mayor Kelley, and, indeed, were not turned back. The verses stood as proof to the claim made in the first verse that activists really would let nobody or nothing turn them around. In the last verse, then, the singers transcended the specifics and refocused their attention beyond the details of the situation, and encouraged listeners to see themselves as capable of withstanding anything that might come in their way. "We Shall Not Be Moved" and "Do What the Spirit Say Do" also progress in this way, to provide activists with detailed lists of their accomplishments, while urging them to persevere.

The singers' strategy of making the abstract concrete was also evident in their descriptions of freedom, descriptions designed to make that abstract concept more real for singers and listeners. These descriptions were important because freedom had been identified as the motive force of the whole movement, the ideal that brought activists together. To better understand their conception of the goal toward which they struggled is to better understand the people who worked for civil rights.

A telling characteristic in the way activists sang about freedom was their description of it as a physical place, a place with tangible characteristics. In "Ain't Gonna Let Nobody Turn Me 'Round" and "I'm On My Way," for instance, activists repeatedly referred to "freedom land," and they sang of "freedom's main line" in "Hallelujah, I'm A-Traveling." In "Michael Row the Boat Ashore," freedom was described as a boat and was also seemingly found in a place "on the other side" of "Jordan River," as it was in "Keep Your Eyes on the Prize." In "We Shall Not Be Moved," the singers claimed "we are fighting for our freedom" and then argued that the fight was succeeding by providing such data, tied to specific, physical changes, as "our parks are integrating" and "we're sunning on the beaches."

In the songs that treated freedom as a place it was common to find it described as a very specific place—heaven. Since the years of slavery in the United States, African-Americans have often drawn an analogy between heaven and freedom, especially in their songs. While some slaves believed that the only freedom they would ever know was the freedom of heaven after death, strong evidence also suggests that when others sang of heaven they were referring to the temporal freedom to be found upon escaping to the North.[4] Civil rights activists continued to use this metaphor of freedom as heaven to sustain their hope and faith by allowing them to describe freedom in concrete terms, but not in terms that could be construed as mundane and uninspiring.

This association between freedom and heaven was made in rather subtle, but multiple, ways in the civil rights songs. Heaven, per se, seems to be mentioned only in "Keep Your Eyes On the Prize," where activists sang:

> Haven't been to heaven but I've been told,
> Streets up there are paved in gold.

Other song lines have many references, however, that would create associations with heaven in listeners' minds, especially where activists had transformed old songs by simply substituting the word "freedom" for "heaven." In earlier black songs, as well as in Christian mythology, heaven is found beyond Jordan River. In the civil rights songs, it is freedom that is to be found over Jordan:

> Jordan River is deep and wide
> We'll find freedom on the other side . . .[5]

> Jordan's river is deep and wide, Alleluja.
> Get my freedom on the other side, Alleluja . . .[6]

The word change, for the activists' purposes, from "heaven" to "freedom" would not erase memory of the earlier wording, which would likely color any interpretation of the new words. Similarly, in the traditional version of "I'm On My Way," singers asserted "I'm on my way to the heavenly land" while civil rights activists adapted the song for their needs, singing "I'm on my way to freedom land."

Thoughts of heaven were also evoked in "I'm Gonna Sit at the Welcome Table," as activists sang of their intention to "walk the streets of glory," another reference usually associated with heaven but here connected to freedom as well. "Jacob's Ladder" would also, presumably, subtly connect the goals of activists to heaven since heaven was the destination of Jacob's ladder. "Going home to my Lord," as mentioned in "Oh Freedom," would likely bring thoughts of heaven; when activists "went home," they would be free. Repeated references in the songs of freedom being "over my head" and "over me" also encouraged a view of freedom as a physical place that might have heavenly associations. As a place, heaven could, perhaps, be related to easily and it might make an inspiring correlation in the minds of activists. Associating freedom with heaven provided a transcendent definition for freedom that made it seem so valuable as to justify any sacrifice made in the achieving.

The singers treated freedom as perceivable by the senses in other notable ways as well. Activists sang of *seeing* freedom in the air, and keeping their eyes on the "prize" of freedom. Likewise, freedom was described as a light that could be seen shining all around.[7] They gave freedom another kind of sensory manifestation when they sang, in "Keep Your Eyes on the Prize," that "freedom's name is mighty sweet." Any one of these references, of itself, would likely have little effect on the listeners' perceptions of freedom, but the degree to which the references appeared, in one form or another and in nearly every song, made it more likely that they combined to argue for a certain view of freedom. Freedom would be real for the activists when the abstract promises made in the United States Constitution and the Emancipation Proclamation found concrete manifestation and could be seen and felt in all areas of black life. The songs suggested that freedom would soon be felt, the intangible made tangible. Freedom was not just an ambiguous, vaguely defined goal, but a state that could be touched and seen and gloried in.

This attention to concrete detail and casting the abstract as tangible was evident in other aspects of the definition of freedom offered by activists in their songs. Activists claimed that freedom meant blacks could act as they wished and do what they desired. Myrna Carter said that, during the 1950s, "freedom was something that we only read about. It was a fantasy, in a sense. We felt that being free was being able to go where you wanted to go, do what you wanted to do, without fear."[8] As the spiritual and literal descendants of slaves, activists conducted most of their protests in the South, where whites continued to limit black freedom. Whites did this in many ways, jailing blacks and issuing injunctions against demonstrations, making it impossible for blacks to register to vote or to be served in restaurants. In songs like "Woke Up This Morning With My Mind on Freedom" and "Do What the Spirit Say Do," activists defined freedom by enumerating the ways that activists could get involved in overturning the restrictions imposed on them in the South. The singers sang of "walking and talking" and "singing and praying" as ways of showing themselves and others that they could and would be free. They also encouraged each other, in "Do What the Spirit Say Do," to take opportunities to prove to themselves that they could march, sing, picket, vote, move, love, and die, if the quest for freedom demanded such action. The abstract word "freedom" gained meaning through the listing of activities that would be available for blacks, and the use of the list amplified the meaning of freedom by providing a multifaceted view of what it meant to be free.

Freedom was also detailed in concrete terms when the singers referred to the conditions preventing freedom and when they urged the removal of them. The attainment of freedom was associated with the end of many negative experiences that blacks had grown to believe were their fate in the American South. In "Oh Freedom," all we know about what freedom *is* is by hearing what it is *not*. The singers defined freedom as "no more segregation," "no more weeping," "no more shooting," "no burning churches," "no more Pritchett" and "no more Jim Crow over me." Significantly, each detail they mentioned was one that blacks endured simply because they were black. The singers asserted that each of these elements oppressing blacks must be removed for the activists to reach the status of other Americans who did not have to be constantly concerned with jailhouses and burning churches.

In "Ain't Gonna Let Nobody Turn Me 'Round," singers also defined freedom by enumerating the obstacles to freedom that must be removed for the "march up to freedom land" to be completed. As in "Oh Freedom," the obstacles were specific people as well as jailhouses, injunctions, and the system of segregation that kept blacks separate and unequal. No other law-abiding American worried about these things and blacks would not be equal, and hence free, until these concerns were removed from their lives as well.

Activists conveyed a worldview in their songs that was built upon their idea of freedom, a blend of abstract and transcendent themes with many vivid and concrete details. On this foundation, they constructed the rest of their description of the world.

THE POWER OF THE SOUTH AS A PLACE

When they defined aspects of their world through song, activists chose to heavily emphasize specific places and locales. They concentrated on the South as a place and, by so doing, the singers referred to shared experiences in such campaigns as Albany or Birmingham, each word being evocative of rich meaning. More important, however, was the way the emphasis on scene created an argument in the songs about the nature of the South, which suggested that the place itself was at the root of the continuing oppression of blacks.

Howard Zinn has written of "the overwhelming power of Southern history,"[9] arguing that the individual Southerner was not so much at fault for the continuing attitudes of racism and bigotry as was the *situation* in the South. Southerners had long lived in a certain atmosphere where

> beyond the physical, beyond the strange look and smell of this country, was something more that went back to cotton and slavery, stretching into history as far as anyone could remember—an invisible mist over the entire Deep South, distorting justice, blurring perspective, and, most of all, indissoluble by reason.[10]

Zinn and others argued that this southern tradition did, indeed, have a power over the behavior of whites in their attitudes toward blacks. Zinn wrote of Harvard sociologist Thomas Pettigrew's concept of the "latent liberal," where Pettigrew described such a person as "the white Southerner who really does not 'feel' prejudice toward the Negro, but who *behaves* as if he does because of the situation around him."[11] The challenge, then, for those who would change white behavior was to change the situation in the South—to change the place.

As Zinn took part in civil rights activities, he believed such a change was possible and, in fact, that it was taking place every day.[12] The lyrics of the freedom songs indicate that the activists understood the power of the place and they, too, believed the place could be changed. When the protestors focused on places, rather than human adversaries, in their songs, they implicitly shifted the blame away from the southern people and suggested that it was, indeed, the situation that was to blame for their continued oppression.

Communication scholar Charles U. Larson suggested, in pursuing a line of reasoning introduced by Kenneth Burke, that when speakers focus on scene they are implicitly suggesting that "changing the scene or environment will change people."[13] The songs of the civil rights movement provide an example of such an emphasis on scene with the activists implicitly arguing that the South could be changed in the fundamental ways necessary for blacks to live as equals with whites. Just as many of the acts of civil disobedience engaged in by civil rights workers involved the occupying of physical spaces in order to claim

them as legitimate places for blacks to be, the songs activists sang made
similar claims to the South as their rightful place.

The extent to which the activists emphasized their place in the
South is especially evident when we contrast their descriptions of it with
the descriptions that were found in the slave spirituals. The spirituals
depicted blacks as eager to leave the land of their mistreatment, in order
to travel toward a better place. Slaves held little hope of changing the
conditions of slavery, so their best hope for a free life involved
removing themselves from the situation. Accordingly, in the songs of
the slaves, we find few references to "here" but many references to the
"Promised Land" and "Canaan," which could be interpreted either as the
heaven of Christian afterlife or as the northern free states to which
many slaves attempted to escape.

In contrast to the spirituals of the slaves, the songs of the civil
rights movement seldom suggested a moving away from the South.
Instead, the activists used their songs to describe the South as belonging
to blacks as well as whites, and suggested ways to change the South.
Activist Fannie Lou Hamer spoke for many when she said "Why should
I leave Ruleville and why should I leave Mississippi? . . . I want to
change things in Mississippi. You don't run away from problems—you
just face them."[14] In Ms. Hamer's favorite freedom song, "This Little
Light of Mine," singers expressed great optimism regarding the potential
for changes to be made in situational elements in the South. In addition
to shining the light of love and freedom on Pritchett and Kelley, the
singers sang of their intent to light the "dark corners" of the land.
References were made to shining the light "deep down in the South,"
"all in the jailhouse," and "down in Birmingham," or Mississippi or
Alabama or wherever the most recent conflicts had occurred.

In "Michael Row the Boat Ashore," the activists focused again on
places, instead of the people who lived there, when they sang:

> Christian brothers, don't you know, Alleluja,
> Mississippi is the next to go, Alleluja.

The verses of "(Everybody Says) Freedom" also drew attention to
places, with such verses as:

> (In the cottonfield) Freedom . . .

> (In the schoolroom) Freedom . . .

(In the jailhouse) Freedom . . .

(All across the South) Freedom . . .

(In Mississippi) Freedom . . .

Similarly, in "If You Miss Me at the Back of the Bus," activists enumerated the many places they were not welcome in the South—the front of the bus, "Ole Miss," the voting booth, the city pool—and described their intention to enjoy them. All of these places, the bastions of segregation and bigotry, were targeted for change and for reclamation.

"Keep Your Eyes on the Prize" was another song in which this pattern of focusing on the locations of racial trouble, instead of people, is evident. No human adversaries were mentioned in this song but there were references to jail, to the "wilderness" from which activists were emerging, and to the towns of the South where activists worked for change. Here again, the implicit focus was on change. The singers recognized that "Albenny Georgia lives in race," but they had resolved to "fight it from place to place."

The changes wrought by the Freedom Riders as they travelled on buses through the towns of the deep South were also offered as testimony in "Keep Your Eyes on the Prize." The Freedom Rides involved activists traveling by bus to the places where they were least welcome in order to establish their rights in those places. The song defined this trip in a telling way. Although the Freedom Rides were punctuated by brutal attacks on the Riders by southern whites, the singers did not focus on these conflicts. The songs did not mention the burning of the bus that carried the first of the Riders through Anniston, Georgia, or the fifty-three stitches needed by Rider Jim Peck when whites had finished beating him. Instead, the singers concentrated on the movement goal of effecting change through the force of brotherly love and positive action:

> We're gonna ride that big Greyhound,
> Carryin' love from town to town.

"Hallelujah, I'm A-Traveling" treated the Freedom Rides, as well as other key black demonstrations, in similar terms. The joy of riding the

Greyhound bus through Mississippi and being able to sit in "the front seat this time" eclipsed the consequences of such an action.

Where black slaves had looked to move far away from the land of their unhappiness, the heirs of their protest in the civil rights movement chose to move through that land and to define it as a place capable of being changed.

In the context of this heavy emphasis on places, the most prevalent place mentioned in the songs was the one in which the singers most often found themselves—jail. The activists had transformed the jail experience from ignoble and fearful punishment into a joyous and fulfilling occasion. Taylor Branch commented on this effect when, in his book, *Parting the Waters: America in the King Years 1954-63*, he wrote of the events connected with the Montgomery bus boycott:

> Some of the arriving smiles were forced, but the ones on leaving jail were always genuine. As the crowd grew into the hundreds, applause and words of encouragement began to lift the mood. . . . Those picked up by deputies . . . passed through the crowd waving and hugging people. Soon the deputies out on the dragnet were coming up empty because so many of the Negroes were on their way downtown voluntarily. Laughter began to spread through the crowd. A joke went around that some inquiring Negroes were upset upon being told by phone that they were not on the arrest list. . . . The jailhouse door, which for centuries had conjured up visions of fetid cells and unspeakable cruelties, was turning into a glorious passage.[15]

John Lewis spoke of the change that came about in the way blacks defined going to jail, saying that, in the past, "to go to jail was to bring shame and disgrace on the family. But for me it was like being involved in a holy crusade, it became a badge of honor."[16] Bayard Rustin, too, commented on the changed attitudes about going to jail, attributing the transformation to Martin Luther King and describing the new recognition that was associated with a trip to jail. As he put it, "Martin made going to jail like receiving a Ph.D."[17] This redefinition of going to jail meant that when whites arrested blacks, they were, in effect, helping blacks and serving their purposes. The activists did not return the favor of cooperating with whites in feeling cowed, unlawful, or ashamed when they went to jail. Being arrested no longer belonged to whites as a punishment for what they saw as wayward blacks; the civil

rights activists had appropriated the experience, redefined it in positive
terms, and made it their own.

Such refusal to respond to white oppression as whites had come to
expect was a large part of black success during the civil rights
movement. Pat Watters, a white reporter who covered many of the civil
rights activities, wrote of what he perceived to be the activists'
realization that they must make crucial changes in themselves. As he
stood and listened to a crowd sing "We Shall Overcome," Watters was
reminded

> of all my life of [my] acquiescence in the evil and *their* acquiescence,
> Negro acquiescence, our mutual acquiescence making the evil seem
> immutable and the South hopeless. . . . I listened and heard them
> saying in the song that the way things used to be was no more, was
> forever ended.[18]

As Watters witnessed, blacks in the civil rights movement were taking
power back into their own hands and redefining themselves. When
blacks changed their self-definition, whites were in the position of
responding to such changes. As a result, the equation of life in the
South changed. The protestors' acts drew outside attention to the
problems in the South and they also served, in large part, to begin to
solve those problems and transform the South.

Although we find many references to jail and know that activists
defined it as a necessary place to go, it is also evident that they
dreamed of the day when these experiences would be behind them.
"Keep Your Eyes on the Prize" highlighted the view of jail as a rite of
passage, in the line that admonishes, "Get off your seat and go to jail."
The same song, however, retained verses from older versions,
celebrating the biblical story of Paul and Silas and their miraculous
escape from the cell. Indeed, this freedom from the jail cell was
associated with the larger freedom for which blacks were struggling, the
freedom that was their "prize." When blacks no longer found themselves
in jail as a result of taking a seat on a bus or requesting service at a
lunch counter, jail could again be defined as a place for lawbreakers,
not the destination of such people as the civil rights activists. In the
meantime, however, protestors sang "we'll all go to jail" and looked
forward to the day when "there'll be no more jailhouse over me."

By concentrating on the scenes of the South, rather than on the
people, the civil rights activists implied that the problems they faced

had as much to do with the locale and a longstanding atmosphere of hate as they did with individual people. They suggested they had the power as a group to change the South, to change the situations that shaped the behaviors of southern people and, by so doing, they argued they could reclaim it as a place welcome to all people.

THE ROLE OF OUTSIDERS

That the activists chose to focus on the South itself, rather than on southern people, is, it would seem, a relatively unusual choice in the strategies of protest rhetoric. Rhetorical critic Richard B. Gregg suggested that protestors, in general, seek to bolster their self-images by the denigration of a perceived adversary,[19] but we find very little evidence of a negative or divisive definition of an "enemy" in the freedom songs.

Consistent with the themes of autonomy and self-reliance stressed in the freedom songs, we find that the songs depicted outsiders in only limited roles. In many of the songs, no mention was made of any person outside the movement circle. The references to "others" in the songs can be categorized in two ways: those who were sympathetic towards the movement and who were, therefore, potential allies, and those who were decisively opposed to the activities for civil rights. Clear distinctions were made in the ways these two types were treated in the songs.

In their songs, activists conveyed consistent optimism regarding the potential for whites to come forward and actively support the movement, in spite of plentiful data attesting to significant white opposition to all attempts for black freedom and equality. Several of the songs expressed irrepressible hope, and encouraged black movement participants to recognize whites as allies, not adversaries. At least three of the songs, "We Shall Overcome," "We Shall Not Be Moved," and "Keep Your Eyes on the Prize," included verses explicitly arguing for cooperation between blacks and whites, and symbolically linking the accomplishment of movement goals to the ability of blacks and whites to work together. These songs were popular ones, sung often, and, with verses like:

We're gonna ride for civil rights,
We're gonna ride both black and white

I know what I think is right,
Freedom in the souls of black and white

and

Black and white together,
We shall overcome,[20]

civil rights workers created a definition of a world in which they could rely on whites to support them and work with them toward shared goals.

The words of many songs also suggested to overhearers that blacks and whites were alike in essential ways, a technique likely to increase white sympathy for the goals of black protestors. For instance, as Sunday-schoolers, many white children are taught, in "This Little Light of Mine," that every person has a little light and is compelled, by virtue of being a Christian, to "let it shine." When civil rights protestors sang this song it was a poignant reminder to whites that blacks struggled to let their lights shine as well.

The singers' emphasis on themes of love and freedom, in songs white listeners would recognize from their own religious experience, provided convincing evidence that protestors were not a threat to whites. If a group could repeatedly assert that they kept their minds "stayed on freedom," they were not likely planning retaliation or looking for ways to assert themselves over others. When singers demonstrated the generosity of spirit evident in verses speaking of the intention to spread love "far and near," to carry "love from town to town," and to "love everybody in my heart," white listeners would be hard pressed to expect animosity from the singers.[21] The songs, in nearly every line, reassured overhearers that blacks did not see their relationship with whites as an adversarial relationship.

The nonthreatening tone of the freedom songs had significant potential appeal for white listeners. Nowhere in the songs did the activists define themselves as militants or marauders for equality; therefore, whites, in their overhearing, were not likely to perceive the movement as one that was designed to promote black causes at the expense of whites. The acquisition of freedom and equality for blacks did not cost whites, according to the songs, but, rather, could be perceived as extending the freedom of all people, including whites.

The songs also argued implicitly for a positive attitude towards whites insofar as the singers avoided any wholesale condemnation of an enemy. Despite the extent to which blacks were subjugated and brutalized by white racists, the songs *never* pointed a finger at the general white population, to repudiate or lay blame. In fact, the enemies of blacks were very seldom mentioned in the freedom songs in any context. Where an adversary was mentioned, it was most often the specific naming of one person—Chief Pritchett, Bull Connor, or Asa Kelley—not a more sweeping accusation.

This choice to name only specific enemies may have encouraged certain attitudes toward whites. By defining their enemies in specific terms, activists avoided the kinds of generalizations and stereotypes their adversaries indulged in when labeling blacks. The approach also localized the issue of opposition. The message was not that "they" are everywhere, out to get us, but rather that a few people posed a problem and were deserving of censure. The songs did not invite listeners to blame the larger population of whites.

The presence of enemies was minimized by the extent to which the singers chose not to make them a central issue in their songs and by the degree to which blacks sang of their own autonomy and power, but the real adversaries of the movement were not entirely ignored nor was their presence denied. Six of the freedom songs named such people as Laurie Pritchett, Asa Kelley, Z. T. Mathews, and Ross Barnett, and named them in contexts that highlighted their commitment to creating obstacles for civil rights activists.[22] Singers used the song "Ain't Gonna Let Nobody Turn Me 'Round" in many situations to respond to the jailings and injunctions that were designed to discourage activists and slow their progress. In this song, singers also featured the specific police chiefs, mayors, and other southern community leaders who used their local power to test the resolve of the protestors.

"Ain't Gonna Let Nobody Turn Me 'Round" provides an example of the tone that the singers often used in commenting on the people who sought to stem the tide of movement activity in the South. The singers seemed almost to respond to the considerable force of their adversaries with a psychic shrug. The adversary was met, was recognized, and was dismissed: "Ain't gonna let Chief Pritchett [Mayor Kelley, Z.T.] turn me 'round." In "Oh Freedom," the singers seemed to look over the obstacles to their goal and, in so doing, rendered the obstacles less fearsome or potent. In the language of faith and certainty, the singers asserted simply that there would be "no more Barnett" and "no more Pritchett over me." The activists recognized attempts to suppress them, but they were not suppressed. They recognized attempts to stop them, but they moved forward. People, jails, court rulings, and segregation itself appeared in the songs only as relatively insignificant obstacles in the inevitable march to "freedom land." By underplaying the adversary in terms of the attention given to them in the songs and the ease with which they could be erased from consideration, the singers redefined formidable enemies in the language of annoying hurdles, easily overcome.

On an even more basic level, the inclusion of the names of some of the more nettlesome whites gave the activists a certain kind of symbolic power. Rhetorical critic Arthur L. Smith made the argument that African Americans "seem to believe that there is some truth in the old adage, 'the namer of names is always the father of things.' To be defined by whites is to remain a slave."[23] One more aspect of the self-definition activists were crafting, then, was to cast themselves as namers. Bernice Reagon recognized the need for this change when she said that "this behavior is new behavior for black people in the United States . . . you call their names and say what you wanted to say."[24] Although this may seem an insignificant accomplishment, it was one more way in which activists used the freedom songs to build a more active, confident attitude towards the people who had oppressed them.

The activists felt strongly that their songs had the potential to affect those who heard them, even if the listeners were adversaries. For instance, Cordell Reagon recalled an incident in Parchman Penitentiary, to which the Freedom Riders were sent after their arrest in Jackson, Mississippi, in 1961. In response to a beating from a guard, a Freedom Rider, with blood on his face, began to sing "We Shall Overcome." According to Reagon, the "guard turned red-faced and walked away."[25] Reagon implied that the singing changed the guard's attitudes towards the protestor, embarrassing or shaming him.

Not all activists saw the singing as likely to shame their opponents. Guy Carawan said simply that the songs could "disarm" opponents of their hostilities, while other commentary stressed a slightly different causal relationship—activists sang and adversaries became less adversarial.[26] Wardens of southern jails, for instance, "seemed to enjoy the singing" and they "actually welcomed us back when we returned to jail," remembered Candie Carawan, who also told the following story:

The day of the first trials in Nashville a crowd of 2500 people gathered around the city court house. Mostly they were Negroes who simply wanted to state by their presence there that they were behind the students and wanted justice. As we waited to go inside we sang:

> "Amen, amen, amen, amen . . .
> Freedom, freedom . . .
> Justice . . .
> Civil Rights . . ." etc.

As Carawan continued to watch, she witnessed behavior surprising to her:

> I looked out at the curb where the police were patrolling, and caught one burley [sic] cop leaning back against his car, singing away—"Civil Rights" . . . He saw me watching him, stopped abruptly, turned, and walked to the other side of the car.[27]

Carawan painted an intriguing picture of a southern lawman caught up in the appeal of singing to such a degree that he found himself singing out for civil rights—a position that may have been in opposition to his conscious attitudes and beliefs. At very least, the police officer's singing seemed inconsistent with his task insofar as he was verbally supporting the people he was assigned to control.

Marilyn Eisenberg also suggested the songs had the potential to soften and persuade even those adversaries who would be most strongly opposed to the tactics of the activists. She said:

> I like to think that these songs had some small effect on others besides the Freedom Riders. Our matron, a formidable looking woman from Alabama, was at first very rough with the girls. She rarely spoke, and although we thought she was sympathetic to us as prisoners, we were sure she hated us as Freedom Riders. But some of the girls, in the true non-violent spirit, saw her as a human being and not as a symbol of authority and oppression. Little by little they began to speak to her. At first it was just "good morning" or "thank you," and then we began to joke with her and have longer and longer conversations. Before I left Parchman she was singing for us on our make-believe radio programs and was often heard humming our freedom songs.[28]

It is revealing that, although the warming of the matron towards the students may have been a result of a variety of influences, Eisenberg attributed the change to the freedom songs specifically. The activists invested the songs with the power to change even the most entrenched segregationists.

In the freedom songs themselves, we see additional references to the activists' conviction that the spiritual force of the movement provided them with the potential to change their opponents in significant ways. "This Little Light of Mine" highlighted the power of love to change conditions in the South, and the references to specific people in this song fell in this pattern. The singers expressed their intention to let their "light of love" shine on Pritchett and on Kelley in order to change them.

The potential for change was also suggested in "Oh Pritchett, Oh Kelley," one of the few songs under consideration here that was ostensibly directed at the opponents of the movement. Addressed to Police Chief Laurie Pritchett and Mayor Asa Kelley, the song beseeched them to "open them cells" and release "God's children." The choice to address a song to these men suggested that the activists could hope that even they were not entirely intransigent.

When activists made few references to movement outsiders in their songs, they took the burden for change upon their own shoulders. Instead of laying blame and attacking outsiders, the singers most often encouraged a positive attitude towards whites and portrayed them as valuable allies. According to the songs, only a few, specific people could be identified as actual adversaries and, even then, those people could have only limited power over the activists if activists continued to respond to them from a position of self-confidence and agapic love. The civil rights activists defined their relationship with whites in positive terms with virtually none of the vituperation critics have come to expect in protest rhetoric.

A WORLD OF OPTIMISM

As the activists spoke of their singing, they also talked about the ways it helped them overcome negative emotions, such as fear and anger, and replace them with love and courage. Many of the references to song concerned the ways singing helped activists to deal with the fear that was their constant companion. Vernon Jordan, then an NAACP official, claimed that "the people were cold with fear until music did what prayer and speeches could not do in breaking the ice."[29] Similarly, Phyllis Martin, a field worker for SNCC, said, the "fear down there is tremendous. I didn't know whether I'd be shot at, or stoned, or what. But when the singing started, I forgot all that."[30] The activists were convinced that "the songs help to dissipate the fear,"[31] and gave the people a way to cope with fear, whenever it returned. Pete Seeger, at a concert in Carnegie Hall on June 8, 1963, called the "best verse" of "We Shall Overcome" the one that says "We are not afraid." He went on, "And, here, you and I up here, like every human being in the world we *have* been afraid, but you still sing it—'We are not afraid. We are not afraid.'"[32] The activists sang when they were afraid, and they represented the singing as their way of facing their fear and banishing it.

The activists claimed to feel so much less afraid when they sang that they began to describe the singing as creating a protective barrier or shield around them. Cordell Reagon remembered his feelings:

> You know you are in trouble, you know you are going to get your butt beaten, you know you are probably going to jail, you know you might even get killed, but the sound, the power of the community, was watching over you and keeping you safe.[33]

Similarly, Bruce Hartford recalled his feelings on a march in Mississippi:

> We were singing. . . . Somehow, I can't explain it, through the singing and the sense of solidarity we made a kind of psychological barrier between us and the mob. Somehow we made such a wall of strength that they couldn't physically push though it to hit us with their sticks. It wasn't visual, but you could almost see our singing and our unity pushing them back.[34]

The activists invested their songs with the power both to remove their unproductive emotions and to protect them from the emotions of others.

Many of the stories about the singing of freedom songs associated it with such emotional strength; the strategy of singing provided activists, in their eyes, with the ability to respond to crisis situations with self-control. In the songs, activists also described a world in which change was imminent and where there was good reason to look to the future with great hope. In the civil rights version of "Over My Head I See Freedom in the Air," "freedom," "victory," and "glory" were described as just out of reach, but within the sight, of the singer. The uplifting tone of this song seems especially significant when we compare it to the song from which it was derived. Originally sung as "Over My Head I See Trouble in the Air," the song was changed by songleader Reagon, who remembered:

> Charlie Jones looked at me and said, "Bernice, sing a song." And I started "Over My Head I See Trouble in the Air." By the time I got to where "trouble" was supposed to be, I didn't see any trouble, so I put "freedom" in there.[35]

That Reagon could claim, during the Albany movement and after the worst episodes of the Freedom Rides, that she saw no "trouble" was testimony supporting the activists' arguments regarding their ability to transcend the difficulties facing them. Similarly, to sing "we are not afraid" and "we shall brothers be" in the face of often fearful opposition encouraged the activists to "keep their eyes on the prize," the ultimate goal of freedom.

While the singers looked forward to the outcome of the movement with great optimism, they spoke candidly about the trials faced by activists. In so doing, however, they described the sacrifice and suffering faced by blacks as closely tied to their dreams for future freedom and equality. The suffering, although real, became subordinated in the songs to the goals of the movement and was most often described as subject to imminent change.

Perhaps the most melancholy of the freedom songs was "Freedom Is a Constant Struggle." Activists sang about their quest for freedom as metaphorically equivalent to "crying," "sorrow," "moaning," and "dying." The references to the states of suffering were repeated, and thus, emphasized in the song, and the song was sung in a minor key. Still, the end of each verse of the song posited that freedom was the inevitable outcome, and reward, of such suffering:

> They say that freedom is a constant struggle,
> They say that freedom is a constant struggle,
> They say that freedom is a constant struggle,
> Oh Lord, we've struggled so long,

We *must* be free, we *must* be free.

The song operated, then, not as a wallow in self-pity, but as a reminder that the trials activists faced had meaning, and that the only way to achieve a goal such as freedom was to be willing to suffer for it.

Other references to the brutal facts of movement involvement—"jail and violence," "burning churches," "suff'rin'"—detailed the trials activists faced, but paired them with references to the end of such oppression. When the singers sang "we've met jail and violence too," they finished by asserting "but God's love has seen us through."[36] The reality of churches burned by racists was admitted but only in the context of relief from such terrorism—"no more burning churches over me."[37] In many songs, like "This Little Light of Mine," the very real possibility of personal injury was recognized but was subordinated to the larger goal of responding to such injury with love for the oppressor:

The light that shines is the light of love . . .

Every time I'm bleeding,
I'm gonna let it shine.

Even the references to the trials of protest were tempered by placing them in the context of the larger spiritual goals of the activists. Theirs was a world where hope and faith were both justified and necessary for effecting change. The vision of the ideal future allowed each setback to be interpreted in the context of a necessary evil in the progress toward freedom. These songs urged listeners to replace fear and sorrow with courage and faith.

SUMMARY

In the songs of the civil rights movement, activists provided a definition of the world for themselves, and invited others to adopt that view. This worldview cast most whites as potential allies, not as adversaries, and focused attention on only a few specific enemies. The singers argued that the scene and situation in the South were more to be faulted than were people, that that situation affected the actions of people, and that the end of segregation and inequality depended on changing the scene. In the worldview asserted by the singers, the desired changes were possible and, indeed, inevitable, if the activists could draw on the inner strength that was part of their self-definition. The definition of the world balanced an accessibility based on concrete details with the inspirational appeal associated with spirituality and abstract goals.

The activists who sang the freedom songs in the civil rights movement used those songs to define themselves in relationship to other people and in relationship to the world in which they lived. We have seen that they described a world and people capable of undergoing the changes necessary if all people were to be free and equal in the South. Consistent with their self-definition as autonomous actors, the activists refrained from laying blame on the shoulders of southern whites and, instead, offered a view of the world in which blacks took responsibility for improving their own lives, while welcoming and encouraging whites to join them.

NOTES

1. Nathaniel Dett, *Religious Folk Songs of the Negro* (Hampton, VA: Hampton Institute Press, 1927), 110.
2. Pete Seeger and Bob Reiser, *Everybody Says Freedom* (New York: W.W. Norton, 1989), 240.
3. From "Do What the Spirit Say Do."
4. James H. Cone, *The Spirituals and the Blues* (New York: Seabury, 1972); Miles Mark Fisher, *Negro Slave Songs* (New York: Atheneum, 1953); John Lovell, Jr., *Black Song: The Forge and the Flame* (New York: Macmillan, 1972).
5. From "Keep Your Eyes on the Prize."
6. From "Michael Row the Boat Ashore."
7. From "Over My Head I See Freedom in the Air," "Keep Your Eyes on the Prize," and "This Little Light of Mine."
8. Myrna Carter in Ellen Levine, ed. *Freedom's Children: Young Civil Rights Activists Tell Their Own Stories* (New York: Avon, 1993), 12.
9. Howard Zinn, *Southern Mystique* (New York: Knopf, 1964), 84.
10. Zinn, *Southern Mystique*, 4.
11. Zinn, *Southern Mystique*, 35.
12. Zinn, *Southern Mystique*, 80.
13. Charles U. Larson, *Persuasion: Reception and Responsibility* (Belmont, CA: Wadsworth, 1989), 133. See also Kenneth Burke, *A Grammar of Motives* (Englewood Cliffs, NJ: Prentice-Hall, 1945).
14. Fannie Lou Hamer in Kay Mills, *This Little Light of Mine: The Life of Fannie Lou Hamer* (New York: Dutton, 1993), 123.
15. Taylor Branch, *Parting the Waters: America in the King Years, 1954-63* (New York: Simon and Schuster, 1988), 177.
16. John Lewis in Henry Hampton and Steve Fayer, *Voices of Freedom: An Oral History of the Civil Rights Movement from the 1950s through the 1980s* (New York: Bantam, 1990), 58.
17. Bayard Rustin in Howell Raines, *My Soul Is Rested: The Story of the Civil Rights Movement in the Deep South* (New York: Penguin Books, 1983), 56.
18. Pat Watters, *Down to Now: Reflections on the Southern Civil Rights Movement* (New York: Random, 1971), 54.
19. Richard B. Gregg, "The Ego-Function of the Rhetoric of Protest," *Philosophy and Rhetoric* 4 (1971): 81-82.

20. From "Keep Your Eyes on the Prize" and "We Shall Overcome."

21. From "This Little Light of Mine," "Keep Your Eyes on the Prize," and "I Love Everybody."

22. It should be noted that one of the important characteristics of the freedom songs was their adaptability. The songs as recorded in the appendix of this book were changed often in the heat of the moment, and activists undoubtedly made references to other specific people, beyond those identified here.

23. Arthur L. Smith, *Rhetoric of Black Revolution* (Boston: Allyn and Bacon, 1969), 9.

24. Bernice Reagon in Hampton and Fayer, *Voices of Freedom*, 108.

25. Cordell Reagon in Bernice Johnson Reagon, "Songs of the Civil Rights Movement 1955-1965: A Study in Culture History" (Ph.D. diss., Howard University, Washington, D.C., 1975), 83.

26. Guy Carawan in Guy Carawan and Candie Carawan, *We Shall Overcome!: Songs of the Southern Freedom Movement* (New York: Oak, 1963), 7.

27. Candie Anderson Carawan in Carawan and Carawan, *We Shall Overcome*, 18; 20.

28. Marilyn Eisenberg in Carawan and Carawan, *We Shall Overcome*, 53.

29. Vernon Jordan in Robert Sherman, "Sing a Song of Freedom," in *The American Folk Scene: Dimensions of the Folksong Revival*, eds. David A. DeTurk and A. Poulin, Jr. (New York: Dell, 1967), 173.

30. Phyllis Martin in Robert Sherman, "Sing a Song of Freedom," 173.

31. Unidentified civil rights worker in Guy Carawan and Candie Carawan, *Freedom Is a Constant Struggle: Songs of the Freedom Movement* (New York: Oak, 1968), 91.

32. Pete Seeger, "We Shall Overcome: The Complete Carnegie Hall Concert," Columbia C2K 45312, re-release, 1989.

33. Cordell Reagon in Seeger and Reiser, *Everybody Says*, 77.

34. Bruce Hartford in Seeger and Reiser, *Everybody Says*, 207.

35. Bernice Reagon in Juan Williams, *Eyes on the Prize: America's Civil Rights Years, 1954-1965* (New York: Viking, 1987), 163.

36. From "Keep Your Eyes On the Prize."

37. From "Oh Freedom."

V

"We Shall Not Be Moved": Defining a Blueprint for Action

In addition to using their songs for self-definition and to translate that definition of self into a broader view of human interaction and of the world, the civil rights activists sang as a way to comment on the avenues of action available to them. In describing themselves as certain kinds of beings, the activists described beings in action. Karen Lebacqz explored the relationship between being and acting:

> Indeed, when we act, we not only *do* something, we also shape our character. . . . And so each choice about what to *do* is also a choice about whom to *be*—or, more accurately, whom to become.[1]

Activists in the civil rights movement, in singing about courses of action to be undertaken and to be avoided, were adding to their evolving rhetorical being and advocating an attitude toward action. An analysis of that attitude provides us with a fuller understanding of whom the activists strove to become.

The participants in the civil rights movement called themselves *activists* but, despite the implications of that noun, when they sang, they described a world in which only limited kinds of overt action were appropriate. Yes, these protestors advocated a path that was relatively more active and involved than those taken by many African Americans prior to the movement, but, consistent with the movement philosophy of nonviolence and civil disobedience, they avoided suggesting actions that could be perceived as revolutionary or adversarial. The songs reinforced the need for a patient, loving course of action while warning listeners away from the extremes of passivity and aggression. The extent to which the songs advocated strong behaviors was surpassed by what we might describe as a call to mental or psychological action.

133

The freedom songs invited an attitude toward acting that parallelled the definitions of the world that emerged from the songs. Activists described their world with a mix of abstract and concrete representations that created a sense of realism and immediacy underpinned by a strong spirituality. Likewise, they blended abstract and concrete recommendations for actions to be taken. While the description of the world was one that emphasized physical places and relatively concrete scenes, however, the descriptions of action in the songs balanced that prosaic tone and imbued the songs with an overriding spiritual tone.

PERSEVERANCE

In the freedom songs, activists issued a call to action consistent with the goals of movement leaders and with the movement's emphasis on countering hate with love. In their songs, the activists repeatedly sang of the need to *believe* and to *love*, and to combine these attitudes in a commitment to perseverance. In fact, perseverance, although it might not seem to qualify as an action, was the behavior activists recommended in many of the songs. Singers made persistence the theme of many of their songs, including, for instance, "Keep Your Eyes on the Prize." The oft-repeated chorus of this song urged listeners to continue in their course: "hold on." Elsewhere, activists sang "there ain't no harm to *keep* your mind on freedom," urged a continued direction, singing "*keep* your eyes on the prize, hold on," and emphasized the need to "stick with the struggle."[2] The implication in these songs, although the past was not explicitly described, was that minds had been on freedom, eyes had focused on the prize for some time, and it was crucially important that this commitment be sustained. Although generations of blacks had yearned to escape the South and to seek better conditions in places where prejudice and hatred had less influence, the civil rights singers urged listeners to remain in the South, to stand firm against outside pressure, and to refuse to yield to attempts to scare activists away from their acts.

The activists featured their intention to persevere in many other songs as well. Just as they defined who they were, in part, by referring to who they were not, they often defined their course of action by telling what they would not do. Among the songs in which activists eschewed certain actions were "We Shall Not Be Moved," "I Ain't Gonna Let Nobody Turn Me 'Round," and "We'll Never Turn Back." In each of these songs, activists refused to bend to white attempts to deter them and emphasized their intention to persevere.

Adopted from the labor movement in the United States and adapted for the cause of civil rights, "We Shall Not Be Moved" strongly asserted the need for activists to stand firm, "just like a tree, planted by the water." Singers provided, as they progressed through the verses in the song, information about the goal from which activists would not be moved and the means for reaching it, and evidence that the movement was accomplishing its goals. The goal, "we are fighting for our freedom," was the topic of the first verse of the song, giving listeners their reason for persevering. As defined by the singers, the "fight for freedom" consisted of working with others, both black and white. This appeal for unity was divided between two verses, the first arguing for the united efforts of black and white:

> We are black and white together
> We shall not be moved. . .

The second of the two verses concerning strategies for achieving the goal of freedom argued for a more general coming together, in the words "we shall stand and fight together, we shall not be moved."

The last verses of "We Shall Not Be Moved" offered evidence that the strategies of standing together and not yielding to outside pressure were accomplishing the goals of the movement. The implicit argument was that, because activists were acting as they were and were persevering, "the government is behind us," "our parks are integrating," and "we're sunning on the beaches." For activists, in this case, *not* doing something accomplished a great deal.

Another popular movement song that used as its theme the unwillingness of activists to yield to outside pressure was "Ain't Gonna Let Nobody Turn Me 'Round." This song was of the type folklorists describe as advancing its theme through incremental change; folksingers call it a "zipper song." It consisted of very simple verses with minimal changes in each verse—a new word could be "zipped in," which detailed the variety of people and tactics that might attempt to obstruct the movement:

Ain't gonna let Chief Pritchett . . .

Ain't gonna let Mayor Kelley . . .

Ain't gonna let segregation . . .

Ain't gonna let no Uncle Tom . . .

Ain't gonna let no fire hose . . .

Ain't gonna let no jailhouse . . .

Ain't gonna let no police dogs . . .

As singers acknowledged the obstacles, however, they simultaneously asserted their intention to overcome such obstacles, and thereby established the capacity of the activists to stand firm in the face of any outside threat, including lawmen and tactics that were seen as immoral and unjust by civil rights workers. The singers created a dialectical opposition between the forces committed to stopping their progress and their own commitment to continuing.

Similar opposition was the theme of "We'll Never Turn Back." Here, singers detailed some of the trials they had already experienced and used them as evidence to support their claim "we'll never turn back." The singers recalled that:

We've been 'buked and we've been scorned . . .

We have walked through the shadows of death . . .

We have served our time in jail . . .

Such treatment had not deterred the protestors, so they could claim "we'll *never* turn back" with confidence in their proven capacity to persevere.

Activists defined their course of behavior, in part, by attesting to their unwillingness to behave as their opponents would like them to, and would expect them to. Blacks in the South had good reason to fear whites and, accordingly, to yield to their demands, yet the civil rights movement was founded on a developing unwillingness among blacks to give up bus seats and the right to vote. "Not turning back" and "not being moved" might seem like modest actions but, in the context of conditions in the American South of the 1950s and 1960s, they were extraordinarily positive and courageous behaviors.

In addition to warnings against giving in to external pressures, the singers warned against internal doubts and emotional reactions capable of undermining the confidence of activists in themselves and the group. Activists seemed concerned about self-doubts they might experience, regarding the validity of their actions. Many verses of the freedom songs were reassuring in tone. In "Woke Up This Morning With My Mind on Freedom," singers sang of freedom as the thing that occupied their waking thoughts and reassured anyone with doubts, saying "there ain't no harm to keep your mind stayed on freedom." The activists' commitment to loving their enemies was not to be doubted either, as they made clear in "I Love Everybody." The activists refused to entertain doubts, regardless of white attempts to raise them:

> You can't make me doubt it . . .
> I love everybody in my heart.
>
> The Klan can't make me doubt it . . .
> I love everybody in my heart.

In the songs, activists argued what they were doing was right and not to be questioned.

A verse of "Keep Your Eyes on the Prize" addressed the morality of black actions, and any doubts about them, by arguing blacks had done only *one* thing wrong—they "stayed in the wilderness a day too long." Conversely, they counteracted that wrong by "the one thing we did right"—starting to fight. In this context, it seems the wilderness metaphor referred to the state blacks had lived in before the movement, when they were isolated from each other and made few attempts to oppose oppression in a systematic way. The singers urged that activists should never doubt the morality of their striving for freedom.

Perhaps one of the most poignant reassurances provided by the freedom songs appeared in "We Shall Overcome." As was common in the freedom songs, verses were added to "We Shall Overcome" when new situations arose and that needed to be addressed. In the face of mounting violence against protestors, singers responded to their own doubts about the value of risking their lives for the movement. William Moore, a white postal worker engaged in a Freedom Walk from

Tennessee to Mississippi, was shot and killed in 1963. Activists added the verse "Moore died not in vain" to "We Shall Overcome" and, by so doing, reassured themselves that the trials they endured in their struggle for civil rights were not endured in vain.

ACTING IN UNITY

In the descriptions of actions, the singers were clear about one thing in particular—"act together," the songs urged. For votes to amass in sufficient numbers or for the jails to be filled, people who had never before imagined themselves making such a stand must come forward. The songs encouraged such people to become involved by assuring them that they were never alone while participating in the movement. Verses like "we'll walk hand in hand," "we shall *all* be free," and "we'll *all* go to jail" focused attention on the need for unity and for mass involvement. The nature of the involvement was defined as a familial one, as singers sang "we shall brothers be" and addressed each other as "Christian brothers." "Brothers, sisters, all" made the ascent up Jacob's ladder, in "I'm on My Way," the singer asked "my brother to come with me" and, in "Up Above My Head," the singer pleaded "if you can't go, let your children go." The use of kinship terms encouraged listeners to respond to activists as they would to members of their family and argued, implicitly, for a connectedness beyond the bonds of friendship or work relations. The civil rights family was an exalted one, working for a transcendent goal. The songs invited all people to join this family, asking only that make they make their voices heard and their presence felt.

Another device used to stress the importance of the unity of activists was evident in "Keep Your Eyes on the Prize." There, singers transformed the meaning of the word "chain" from a negative one, associated with the chains of slavery, to a positive one, but with special meaning. They sang:

> The only chain that a man can stand,
> Is that chain of hand in hand.

The image of people uniting in a chain of brotherhood was an evocative one that spoke of people working together but that also represented those people as inextricably bound together by the chain. Implicit in such a metaphorical use of the word "chain" is the understanding that any chain is only as strong as is its weakest link. For the movement to remain strong, the songs argued, individuals must begin to see themselves as strong, resilient links in a cooperative effort.

The freedom songs defined unified action as an essential means to the end of freedom. In some songs, activists defined the nature of unification more specifically. True freedom, they asserted, was attainable only when blacks worked together with whites, and vice versa. In both "We Shall Overcome" and "We Shall Not Be Moved," singers explicitly advanced this claim:

> Black and white together,
> We shall overcome,

and

> We are black and white together,
> We shall not be moved.

By so doing, activists associated their chances for freedom with their ability to work with whites. The songs recommended against alienating whites and implied that whites, and the white power structure, could and should be included in black strategies for attaining their goals.

PSYCHOLOGICAL PREPARATION FOR ACTION

In the place of self-doubt and negative emotions, the songs of the civil rights movement urged activists to practice love and patience, and to engage in mental preparation for dealing with the violence and opposition they would face. The emphasis in the songs was often on psychological or emotional verbs instead of behavioral verbs. A careful analysis of the freedom songs also indicates that, when activists sang of their feelings and emotions, they most often cast their thoughts in the past and present tenses. As we shall see, when the activists turned their commentary to behaviors, they sang in the future tense. This, too, suggests that activists felt they were engaging in mental preparation to enable them to proceed in more overtly active ways.

Remarkably few verses in the freedom songs contained any direct reference to the past, so the songs avoid any strong sense of blame for oppression or of regret. In only six songs, "Keep Your Eyes on the Prize," "This Little Light of Mine," "Woke Up This Morning With My Mind on Freedom," "Hallelujah, I'm A-Traveling," "We'll Never Turn Back," and "Freedom Is a Constant Struggle," did verses refer to a time before the movement or earlier in it.

Singers repeated the words "I woke up this morning with my mind on freedom," which attested to the prominence that thoughts of freedom had achieved in their lives in the very recent past. In "Keep Your Eyes on the Prize," two verses summed up past actions and the realization that a change had begun:

> The only thing that we did wrong,
> Stayed in the wilderness a day too long.
>
> But the one thing that we did right,
> Was the day we started to fight.

This song subtly invited singers to acknowledge their own role in the racial problems but shifted attention quickly to the positive change they had since made. The words left the nature of the "fight" ambiguous, so the verses focused attention more on the thought processes involved in the weighing of past actions rather than on the actions themselves.

The section of "This Little Light of Mine" sung in the past tense referred to no specific action by the singers. The second bridge of the song enumerated gifts given by God to the activists, gifts the activists were then to use in their struggle. The gifts related primarily to psychological states:

> On Monday he gave me the gift of love
> Tuesday peace came from above
> Wednesday he told me to have more faith
> Thursday he gave me a little more grace
> Friday he told me just to watch and pray
> Saturday he told me just what to say
> Sunday he gave the power divine—
> To let my little light shine.

The use of the past tense here created the impression that the activists had arrived in the present in possession of the emotional and spiritual strengths necessary to respond nonviolently and lovingly in adverse situations. The bridge provided a frame of reference, then, for the verses in the song. The verses were cast primarily in the future tense and detailed the kinds of actions protestors were prepared to undertake because of the emotional preparation already undergone.

The verses of "We'll Never Turn Back" were also cast in the past tense and juxtaposed the trials endured by activists with the promise made in the chorus:

> We have walked through the shadows of death.
> We've had to walk all by ourself.
>
> We have served our time in jail
> With no money for to go our bail.
>
> But we'll never turn back,
> No we'll never turn back,
> Until we've all been free and we have equality.

In "Freedom Is a Constant Struggle," activists also sang of the long ordeal faced by African-Americans, saying:

> Oh Lord, we've struggled so long . . .
> Oh Lord, we've cried so long . . .
> Oh Lord, we've died so long . . .

These burdens of the past, as related by the singers, reminded activists, if any reminder was needed, of the source of their discontent and the need for their continued work.

The few references to the past provided only the vaguest sketch of what had brought activists to their present state. They had experienced some difficulties of unidentified origin, had recognized the need to respond, and were in possession of the spiritual strengths necessary to ensure a positive response. In their songs, activists suggested that what had happened in the past was less interesting than their present endeavor and plans for the future.

In songs commenting on the present, activists continued to describe themselves as "thinkers" and "feelers" more than as "do-ers." Verses claiming an absence of the negative feelings of fear and loneliness have been noted. This was one way activists communicated about their current states of mind and demonstrated mental and emotional preparedness for the task at hand—they would face the future unafraid and not alone. The words sounded with conviction the protestors' commitment, in heart and mind, to their cause.

In the present tense, activists sang of what they knew ("I know what I think is right," "Christian brothers, don't you know"),[3] what they desired ("we want justice," "freedom's name is mighty sweet")[4] and what they felt ("I'm gonna love," "I love everybody," "stand up and rejoice").[5] In some songs, the activists included two verbs alluding to mental activity in one statement. For instance, in "We Shall Overcome," verses were often sung with the line "I know that I do believe" and "Keep Your Eyes on the Prize" included the words "I know what I think is right." In all of these instances, activists focused on internal states, not overt action.

Other references to the present reflect an image of people in transition—clear in their minds about their goals but not yet meeting them. Activists sang with conviction that "deep in my heart, I do believe," "I feel the fire burning," "we want freedom," and "I know freedom is a-comin'," but sang little about actions they were engaged in at present.[6] They talked about current obstacles, detailing that "churches are burning," "someone's shooting," and "Jordan River is chilly and cold"[7] and implied they would overcome them since "I see freedom in the air" and "we've got the light of freedom."[8] They urged that choices be made by asking "which side are you on?" and admonishing "you're either for the Freedom Rides or a Tom for Ross Barnett."[9] Even the more behavioral actions they claimed to be presently involved in were transitional; they sang about being in the middle of things when they said "hallelujah, I'm a-travelin'," "I'm on my way," and "we are climbing."[10] These fairly vague behaviors were always presented in terms of the singer's involvement, as if to set an example for others.

The protestors sang of their thoughts and beliefs, and they also described their efforts to share those ideas. In the freedom songs, activists often described their present state as one in which communicating about their goals and envisioning the ideal future were important tasks. Several songs contained lines referring to talking about freedom and, of course, when they talk, "everybody says freedom." Sometimes the communicating was given religious tones, as singers referred to the praying in which they engaged and their willingness to preach, if necessary. The importance of singing was not overlooked, as activists described their "singing and praying with my mind on freedom," and urged each other, in "Michael Row the Boat Ashore," to continue singing. In "Keep Your Eyes on the Prize," however, activists made reference to their tradition of singing as only a starting point:

> Singing and shouting is very well,
> Get off your seat and go to jail.

In so doing, they made explicit what was suggested in their songs, as they referred to past, present, and future—the time was coming when they must be willing to take greater risks and become more involved in direct action.

The internal states advocated by activists were represented as being closely related to the attainment of freedom. Freedom was dependent, according to movement philosophy, on the activists' ability to maintain their love and commitment; a nonviolent stance was possible only for activists who were spiritually and temperamentally capable of restraint and unlimited fellowship for other people. The philosophy of nonviolence informed the actions of activists and, concomitantly, the acts protestors engaged in, and their communication about such actions, reinforced their self-image as people deserving of freedom. The tone of love and brotherhood was so strong in these songs that there can be little doubt that activists conceived of their struggle as one on the side of angels, and believed it could be fought by using gentler, subtler weapons than were used against them.

Even the type of songs chosen for use in the movement emphasized emotion more than action. According to classifications made by folklorists, the freedom songs fall into the category of lyric folksongs, songs featuring a first person point of view and not primarily concerned with telling a story, as are ballads. Lyric folksongs are characterized as amorphous and are easily changed by the addition or deletion of verses that suit a particular situation or audience.[11] Such songs "tend to be assemblages of conventional stanzas which could go in any order without harming the feeling. In other words, where ballads and dialog songs call for a movement to dramatize, lyrics involve only the force of mood."[12] The freedom songs were clearly lyric in nature. The songs seldom took the form of narratives, and one of the characteristics that made them especially useful to activists was the ease with which verses could be changed to adapt a song to a specific civil rights campaign.

Folklorists argue that lyric songs stress the "private experience, the emotional dimension" and that the effect of this emphasis on emotion is that action is slowed down or arrested, while emotion and mood is explored.[13] In addition, the heavy repetition of verses and lines evident in the freedom songs also served to slow action and to enhance the feeling that a song was more focused on emotion than on action.[14] Such song forms do not convey a sense of urgency toward action, but rather create and sustain an emotional attitude or mood towards the issues and, in the civil rights songs, toward the endstate of freedom. The use of lyric songs served to promote an attitude toward freedom, more so than providing concrete information about how to achieve the goal.

To say the singers stressed mental actions and emotions is not to suggest they recommended passivity or compliance. The mental states championed in the songs were proactive, positive responses to situations that invited negative reactions. That activists chose to express themselves in this way implies their conviction regarding the necessity of such a strong psychological foundation. If activists were to engage in the behavioral actions deemed strategically sound by leaders of the movement, they must prepare themselves emotionally and psychologically for such action. It is perhaps most appropriate to call this preparation a kind of acting in its own right, the act of continuing to believe when the odds were against the activists, and the act of continuing to love when other people persisted in being most unlovable.

BEHAVIORAL ACTIONS

The songs, in their combination of past and present tenses, suggested that activists had arrived at the present psychologically prepared to take the next step toward freedom. They would not dwell on the past, and were presently full of love, faith, and the desire for freedom. Most of the comments referring to behavioral action, then, were cast in the future tense, in the form of what "I'm gonna do" or what "we shall/will do." It was in the future tense that activists generally referred to the actions of voting, riding a freedom bus, or going to jail. These references to concrete, physical actions took the future-oriented forms of intentions for personal actions or instructions to others about their actions ("you gotta do").

This use of the future tense might have had the effect of casting the proposed actions in some doubt because they were only *proposed* actions. In the songs, however, the singers so consistently used strong terms of intent that they conveyed a sense of inevitability about their propositions. Never do we see any qualifiers about intent, nothing that hedges about what "we *should* do" or what *might* happen. Rather, the singers repeatedly asserted "I'm *gonna* ride," "I'm *gonna* vote," "I'm *gonna* get my civil rights" or "sit at the welcome table" or "march." The listener was provided with an image of the human being striving to change and destined to succeed. To the same end, they sang of what "we *will* do" or, even more strongly, what "we *shall* do."

The choice of the word "shall" is an interesting one because, in the context of standard language choices of oral English, "shall" stands out as unusual. The much more common word used to refer to intentions is "will" and, in fact, "We Shall Overcome" was derived from an earlier protest song that asserted "We Will Overcome." To borrow phrasing from Arnold, the word "shall" is "specially 'reserved' in English"; it *means* differently than does "will."[15] Because it is relatively unusual, the word "shall" lent emphasis to the meaning conveyed, a meaning containing a sense of determination and inevitability beyond the meaning conveyed by the simple futurity of "will." The appeal for protestors of such a stress on the inevitable accomplishment of their goals is not hard to fathom. A seemingly small consideration, "shall" was repeatedly used in both "We Shall Overcome" and "We Shall Not Be Moved," with a consequent accretion that communicated differently, and more effectively, for civil rights activists than would the more common choice of words.

The stress on the inevitable was one that was likely to give activists hope for the outcome of their actions. It also provided additional information regarding a definition of self. To claim with certainty that "I'm gonna walk the streets of glory" implied a definition of the self as worthy of reward, whether we interpret "streets of glory" as a traditional religious destination or as the localized and secularized streets of an integrated South. The conviction with which protestors raised their voices to claim "we shall all be free" implicitly defined the singers as strongly committed and enormously self-confident. Little in the day-to-day developments of the movement would encourage a strong belief in such claims, but activists continued to sing about their goals, demonstrating their level of commitment and their belief in themselves.

While the activists believed in the inevitability of their success, they recognized that change was likely to be slow in coming and in their songs they reminded themselves to be patient. The songs legitimated a slow, steady advance with singers urging actions consistent with the nonviolent philosophy of movement leaders. This attitude of patience and forbearance grated on some, but activists seemed to have felt a need for a realistic appraisal of their progress. Lillian Hellman complained to Pete Seeger about "We Shall Overcome," as an anthem of the movement saying, "You call that a revolutionary song? What kind of namby-pamby, wishy-washy song is that? Mooning, always 'Some day, so-o-me-day!' That's been said for two thousand years." When Seeger raised this concern to Bernice Reagon, she responded, "Well, if we said we were going to overcome next week, it would be a little unrealistic. What would we sing the week after next?"[16] The songs reflected the slow, steady forward movement of the marches and urged the accomplishment of change through the established channels of voting and trusting the government, in addition to engaging in approved acts of civil disobedience.

The activists went further to complement their calls for psychological and emotional commitment to the movement with arguments for more overt, physical behaviors as well. If a protestor wondered "what can I do?," the songs suggested a variety of positive, nonviolent actions. Activists were urged "you gotta sing," "you gotta move," and "you gotta march." The struggle of the civil rights activists took the form of "walkin' and talkin'," and "singin' and prayin'" for freedom.

When activists referred to physical action, they very often concentrated on what seem to be the most mundane activities. Although the occasional verse urged "you gotta die when the spirit says die," the songs were much more likely to recommend walking, talking, marching, singing, and praying. These were the behaviors people engaged in every day as they simply lived their lives and, as such, might seem rather pathetic when offered as the ways to spark a fundamental change in the South. The singers transformed these homely acts, even glorified them, by defining them as the keys to achieving their transcendent goal of freedom. In the songs, there was no such thing as simple movement. Walking and marching were invariably "up to freedom land" and traveling led "down freedom's main line."[17] The activists' songs and prayers were inspired by freedom ("singing and praying with my mind stayed on freedom") and, in fact, to stop singing was to doom the movement:

> Michael's boat is a freedom boat, Alleluja.
> If you stop singing then it can't float, Alleluja.[18]

The activists sought to reward all levels of involvement and defined all action as action that could benefit the cause. When undertaken in the name of freedom, there were no small acts.

Other than references to walking, talking, marching and singing, there appeared relatively few concrete calls to specific action in the songs. In several songs, activists referred to jail as a reality to be faced in movement life, but a willingness to go to jail was actually argued for in only two songs. In "We Shall Overcome," the singers claimed that part of the ability to overcome was dependent on the assumption that "we'll all go to jail." A verse of "Keep Your Eyes on the Prize" suggested that going to jail was a necessary step to be taken beyond the less costly and less intimidating acts of singing and marching:

> Singing and shouting is very well
> Get off your seat and go to jail.

Other songs referred to jail but not in the context of calling protestors to that action, specifically. In "(Everybody Says) Freedom," singers associated going to jail with being free in oxymoronic fashion when they sang, "(In the jailhouse) Freedom, freedom, freedom." They cast their experiences in jail in the past tense in "We'll Never Turn Back," singing "we have served our time in jail." The wording of this song, and others, made the jail time seem a rite of passage for activists and, in the context of the civil rights movement, as we know, going to jail had been redefined as a valued nonviolent strategy. The songs encouraged listeners to view going to jail as a positive act but generally did not argue strongly that all activists must, themselves, go.

Spending time in jail was among the most unconventional and daring of the actions undertaken by civil rights activists. Other related acts, which led to the arrest of protestors and to attacks on them, were the Freedom Rides and the sit-ins at segregated facilities. These actions, although they involved many protestors, were not heavily stressed in the songs. The only direct references to sitting in, in the songs as they are under consideration here, appeared in "I'm Gonna Sit at the Welcome

Table" and "Hallelujah, I'm A-Traveling." In "I'm Gonna Sit at the Welcome Table," singers stated their intention to make every public table in the South a "welcome table." The key to accomplishing this was, in part, sitting at segregated restaurants, as the activists asserted when singing, "I'm gonna sit at Woolworth's lunch counter." "Hallelujah, I'm A-Traveling" treated the sit-ins in the past tense and cited them as examples of the success activists had achieved with direct action.

The Freedom Rides, likewise, were seldom the focus of the songs. They were alluded to in one verse of "Keep Your Eyes on the Prize," as activists sang:

> We're gonna board that big Greyhound,
> Carryin' love from town to town.

The singers, here, shifted emphasis away from the pragmatics of the opposition activists faced to a very different orientation—the Freedom Rides were defined as the act of carrying love through the South. The Rides received more attention in "Hallelujah, I'm A-Traveling," a song designed to be sung on the Rides. Singers of this song did not direct listeners to participate in the Rides but, rather, cast the song as an individual report of involvement and celebration of accomplishment. Neither sitting in nor participating in the Freedom Rides was strongly advocated in the songs as a specific means to an end.

The activists also gave some attention to voting and implicitly urged listeners to work within the established system in the United States. Many movement leaders argued that the key to change in the South was creating a substantial black voting bloc with the potential to elect black officials and force white leaders to more seriously consider black issues. The act of voting was offered as a positive step to be taken in "Do What the Spirit Say Do," "This Little Light of Mine," and "If You Miss Me At the Back of the Bus." In the former, listeners were urged "you gotta vote when the spirit say vote," in addition to praying, singing, loving, and dying when the "spirit say do." Similarly, in "This Little Light of Mine," the singers enumerated the places where they must shine their lights and declared that when "voting for my freedom, I'm gonna let it shine." In "If You Miss Me At the Back of the Bus," activists sang of voting as one of several specific behaviors that would signify the success of the movement:

If you miss me in the cotton field,
And you can't find me nowhere,
Come on down to the courthouse, I'll be voting right there.

The freedom songs did not consistently offer one or two particular actions as the key steps for protestors to take. Rather, they provided a variety of outlets that ranged from the relatively nonthreatening singing and walking to the bolder sitting in and going to jail. In this scope, the diverse participants in the movement could find their own ways to proceed and their own ways to contribute.

Although the songs did not strongly urge every activist to go to jail or to the picket line, they seem to have encouraged an attitude toward action and suggested that each person could progressively become more actively involved. The use of language, including shifts between past, present, and future tenses in these songs, implicitly argued that something of importance had begun in the South and that it was the responsibility of activists to sustain and advance the cause. As a rule, when activists sang of the past and the present, it was mostly about their emotions and psychological attitudes. When they looked into the future, however, they were more likely to sing confidently about *actions* that would be taken.

The singers of the freedom songs described themselves as people who possessed, and were drawing on, an enormous capacity to love and to believe in themselves and in their dreams. When they sang of the present, they implied they had reached a state of mental and psychological preparedness for further, overt action. When they sang about potential action, activists they allowed themselves to become comfortable with the ideas of going to jail and registering to vote, and were thereby able to try them out symbolically before actually engaging in them.

Whether the behavior engaged in was relatively cautious or more daring, in all cases activists described themselves as changing. These changes in self, it was suggested, would act as the catalyst that would put an end to the power that others held over blacks. With their emphasis on the future, the activists committed themselves to continued change.

TRANSCENDENCE

The theme of change was prominent in both the activists' comments about their singing and in the lyrics of the songs. Activists made it apparent that the transformation they saw themselves undergoing was not merely change but transcendence. They argued for a course of action by which they transcended the day-to-day ugliness of the situation they faced in the South, and rise above the hatred directed at them instead of responding to it.

Roderick P. Hart, in a discussion of Burkeian analysis, provided a useful distinction between Kenneth Burke's concepts of hierarchy and transcendence. He said that "hierarchy argues that people can get more; transcendence argues that they can become better."[19] Certainly, when people became involved in the civil rights movement and risked their college careers, their jobs, and their lives, they did so in the hope that their sacrifices would help blacks get more. When civil rights leaders planned the 1963 March on Washington, the name they gave it revealed their dual goals—it was the March on Washington for Jobs and Freedom. In their freedom songs, however, the activists chose to describe their mission by arguing they could become better people. All else was secondary.

That the activists saw themselves as transcending the situation they faced in the South is evident in the language choices they made in describing their singing, as well as in the songs lyrics. In describing the transformation they underwent when they sang, they spoke of "revival," "renewal," "achievement," and of the "new step" they were taking to reach a "new level" and a "higher level."[20] The songs were referred to as the key that allowed activists to unlock certain areas in their lives and enabled them to rise above difficulties. Willie Peacock suggested that, by singing, "you release your soul force" while Jane Stembridge cast singing as the way people found effective for "releasing their common vision."[21] For Hollis Watkins, singing was what enabled him to transcend the fears and negative feelings he faced during the movement. For him, "you sing to throw off weight, your burden. When you are weighted down and your spirit is low, your mental capacity is low. But when you sing, and you let go of that weight, you rise up."[22] Even when Watkins spoke of relaxing during the movement, he referred to singing, when he would "let those songs lift me, lighten me."[23] A frequent use of the word "evolution" combined both the sense of a natural order and the moving ahead to something better.[24] In all of these references, activists associated the singing of the freedom songs with a sense of "becoming." The songs, according to the activists, enabled them to release the best parts of themselves, to rise up, to become.

Activists described the change occurring in them as enabling them to rise above common human fears and negative emotions. Activists related their accounts of the movement, and featured the emotional and physical strength they drew from their singing. For instance, Dorothy Cotton wrote of her confrontations, as a part of a group of activists, with Hoss Manucy in St. Augustine:

> After we were attacked we'd come back to the church, and somehow always we'd come back bleeding, singing "I love everybody . . ." It was hard. . . .Then somebody would always stop, because it was hard to sing "I love Hoss Manucy" when he'd just beat us up, to say a little bit about what love really was. He's still a person with some degree of dignity in the sight of God, and we don't have to like him, but we have to love him. He's been damaged too. So we sing it, and the more we sing it, the more we grow in ability to love people who mistreat us so bad.[25]

Cotton accorded enormous power to the singing in which she and others engaged, and suggested that, although they met with great provocation to respond to their adversaries in anger, the act of singing gave them the strength to transcend that all-too-human emotion and to resist the instinct to respond.

The memories of other activists add evidence to the singers' claims that their singing provided them with a special ability to rise above the actions of their foes. Seeger and Reiser recount the reaction of a young boy who enacted the words he was singing, even in the face of physical abuse:

> One fourteen-year-old said, "We was singing 'I love everybody,' and one of them stuck me with a cattle prod and said, 'You don't love everybody,' and I said, 'Yes, I do.'"[26]

Bob Zellner described another such confrontation in which demonstrators chose to respond to violence with the nonviolence of song:

The march was stopped about a block and a half from the campus by 40 city, county, and state policemen with tear gas grenades, billy sticks and a fire truck. When ordered to return to the campus or be beaten back, the students, confronted individually by the police, chose not to move and quietly began singing "We Shall Not Be Moved."[27]

Julius Lester also remarked on the emotional strength he asserted singers received from their songs, saying that:

The new songs serve much the same function as the old. The freedom songs give the people courage to walk down the streets of Birmingham and face the dogs that are trained to kill on command. In Nashville, Tennessee, the students, returning from a demonstration, had to march up the center of the street between a mob which lined both sides. While the mob threw rocks and bottles at them, they sang "We Shall Overcome." This was not a pretentious display of non-violence. The song was simply their only recourse at a time when nothing else would've helped.[28]

Both Zellner and Lester stressed the ways that the songs provided the emotional wherewithal to maintain a nonviolent stance, manifested through both physical and emotional discipline. By singing, activists advertised their ability to embody the nonviolent philosophy that was so important in the movement. Through their songs, and other forms of direct action, activists translated the abstract concept of nonviolence into their daily lives. Wayne Hampton argued that "the protest singers of twentieth-century America believed they were armed with a weapon more powerful than guns and bombs. And they felt that they had no need to resort to violence. Music cannot be used violently."[29] Whether or not Hampton is correct about music's nonviolent potential, it is valid to say that music was not used by blacks in an angry or violent manner in the civil rights movement. Music was one alternative to force, one that was implemented repeatedly in the many stages of the movement.

Singing was also important because it provided the activists with something to *do* in response to the violent acts of their adversaries. The singing provided an outlet, a preplanned strategy of acting in a pacifist but nonpassive way. All forms of nonviolent direct action, including music, are what Ralph H. Turner called "positive action, not mere passivity."[30] These acts provided an important kind of equipment for living, an active alternative to violence. While whites often acted against blacks with seemingly uncontrolled physical violence, blacks strove to find ways to remain in control and to make conscious choices while presenting themselves in the best light. The songs, well known to all, became scripts easily drawn upon to replace the urge to react in kind to violence. With their songs, activists had the opportunity to retain power and act according to their own values and goals rather than giving power to the segregationists by reacting to their provocations in negative, damaging ways. By means of their singing, the activists felt they found the strength, in the words of Martin Luther King, Jr., to "meet physical force with soul force."

Themes of transcendence were evident in the lyrics of the freedom songs as well, with transcendence portrayed as the ultimate spiritual act in which protestors could engage. The activists described themselves as acting in ways that set them above the ordinary. The very atmosphere in which activists lived was described in terms contributing to this effect, and singers emphasized vertical movement as well, by relating their efforts to reach up and over the trials they faced. Freedom, glory, and victory were "in the air" and "over their heads." Freedom filled every waking thought and their eyes beheld their prize. The light of freedom in "This Little Light of Mine" shone from above and "every rung" of Jacob's ladder went "higher, higher." In "Oh Freedom," freedom was repeatedly described as "over me" and was associated with a heavenly state. In "Ain't Gonna Let Nobody Turn Me 'Round," the singers refused to let anything or anyone deter them from their march "up to freedom land."

In all of these references to vertical movement, up and over the current situation, a definition of self as capable of transcendence accrued. The activists sang, as well, of love and argued consistently for selfless love and for treating adversaries in ways that transcended the all-too-human desire for retaliation. In order for the movement goal to be attained, blacks argued they must earn it by discipline and spiritual transcendence.

By making freedom and love, ultimate terms, stand for all their more specific hopes and desires, activists translated all of their acts into something special. Riding a Greyhound bus became a transcendent act because activists described that act in transcendent terms. Why did they ride the bus? To gain the right to travel on the buses without harassment and to be treated in the same way as whites? Not according to "Keep Your Eyes on the Prize." The reason given in the song for riding the Greyhounds was to "carry love from town to town." And why go to jail? To demonstrate that blacks no longer feared this form of white control? To draw the attention of the government and American people to the abuse of the judicial system in the South? Perhaps, but in "This Little Light of Mine," activists suggested they were going to jail in order to let the "light of love" shine even there.

In "We Shall Overcome," activists focused their attention entirely on transcendence. It might be argued that the use of the word "overcome" was a chancy one in the context of a self-proclaimed nonviolent movement, inviting, as it might, interpretations associated with an antagonistic or confrontational attitude toward a human enemy. But, because the song was sung as one of many freedom songs, in the context of nonviolent philosophy, and because of the common American usage of the word "overcome," the likely interpretation was a nonthreatening one.

The way the word "overcome" is commonly used suggests that "We Shall Overcome" was not about blacks defeating whites. We generally talk about "overcoming hardships" or "overcoming the odds against us," primarily in reference to the surmounting of difficulties rather than to trouncing a human adversary in a contest. Human beings may be a part of creating the hardships to be overcome but the obstacles themselves are more abstract and seem to admit to a situational complexity that cannot be easily pegged on a scapegoat figure. Additionally, when we refer to someone's overcoming of hardships, it does not really suggest that the obstacles have been removed or somehow dismantled, but rather that the person has risen above them through perseverance and strength of character. In other words, to "overcome" means quite literally to "come over," to transcend or to rise above.

Other elements encouraged an interpretation of "We Shall Overcome" as nonthreatening to outsiders as well. We find the absence of any named enemies typical of the freedom songs. No individual was ever specified as the obstacle to be overcome, nor were whites mentioned in a more general, adversarial sense. In fact, the only reference to "outsiders" in the song defined them, in effect, as insiders, as activists sang "black and white together, we shall overcome." The overcoming referred to here was not the overcoming of people, but of something larger.

As activists sang of overcoming, they argued that they must transcend their acceptance of a limiting white definition of blacks and that they must transcend the institutionalized racism pervasive in the South. To do so, they must learn not to fear or, at least, not to allow their fear to hinder them ("we are not afraid"). They also must learn not to think of themselves as isolated and powerless ("we are not alone"). Instead, the quest must be undertaken by the group ("we'll walk hand in hand") and must include a relationship with whites ("black and white together"). The singers offered proof of the moral rectitude of their struggle, couched in the terms of transcendence, as well—they had both "the truth" and "the Lord" on their sides. The key to transcendence, according to the song, was the activists' belief in themselves and in the positive outcome of their striving:

> Oh-oh, deep in my heart,
> (I know that) I do believe,
> (Oh) we shall overcome someday.

The voicing of such intentions and commitment was important to the movement because the articulation of intentions is a crucial step in carrying out those intentions. We become committed or involved when we *say* we are, when we articulate our intentions for others to hear. The presidential oath of office, wedding vows, citizenship ceremonies, and the pledge of allegiance to the American flag are examples of circumstances in which we believe that verbalization transforms a person from one state of being to another.

Singing in the civil rights movement offered an outlet for voicing commitment available to all. Each person who sang was more likely to perceive his or her role in the movement as important and the public articulation of intentions made the individual less likely to desert the movement. As Larson argued, "when a person describes to us what they intend to do, they have, in a sense already symbolically enacted the behavior."[31] And once people had become involved to the extent of raising their voices in song, there was the potential they would build on that involvement and become increasingly committed and willing to lend support in other ways.

Larson referred to "enactment," a concept discussed by Campbell and Jamieson as well, who described it as a "reflexive form . . . in which the speaker incarnates the argument, *is* the proof of the truth of what is said."[32] Such enactment was a large part of the appeal of singing in the civil rights movement. Many people who attended only to the words of "We Shall Overcome" worried that the song encouraged an attitude of gradualism because it explicitly described a state that was aspired to, a goal that would be reached "someday," and gave limited information about *how* it might be achieved. What is overlooked in such an analysis, however, is that, through the act of singing, the civil rights activists implicitly argued that their goal was already reached.

In what may seem a paradox, as the singers stated their intention to overcome, they simultaneously identified themselves as people capable of overcoming *and*, in so doing, demonstrated the extent to which they had already surmounted many of the obstacles facing them. By marching and singing in spite of all that southern whites would do to prevent such demonstrations, blacks *had* overcome. By perceiving that many whites would choose to stand with activists and against the likes of Bull Connor, blacks *had* overcome. By refusing to be dragged down by the violence saturating the South and hampering the movement, and by transcending their impulses to fight back in kind, blacks *had* overcome. As the singers articulated their aspirations, they were implicitly asserting that they had already attained much to which they claimed to aspire. The act of singing stood as proof to the claims made in the songs. What was argued through content was being enacted as already true. They *were* working, black and white together; they *were* no longer afraid; they *were*, by personal commitment and a seemingly suprahuman love, transforming themselves and the entire South.

SUMMARY

The blueprint for action the protestors provided for themselves was a complex one. They sang of the value of preparing themselves mentally and psychologically for action and concentrated on the emotional strengths necessary to sustain them. They also recommended more specific behaviors for future consideration as long as those behaviors derived from the correct spiritual stance and were motivated by transcendent goals. In all ways, the activists defined their actions as transcendent acts. They were motivated, as they described it, by freedom and love and the desire to become better people. Such a description was likely to remove doubts activists held about the propriety of civil disobedience and cast the civil rights movement into terms appealing to observers of the struggle as well.

CONCLUSION

This has been a study of symbolic redefinition, of the ways a group of people replaced a limiting definition of self with a liberating one. Civil rights activists used their songs to define themselves and their place in the world they were seeking to change. In their definition of self, the activists sought to refute the predominating white definition of southern blacks. The activists chose to stress descriptions of themselves as autonomous individuals who had joined their efforts to achieve freedom for all blacks in America. They defined themselves as capable of responding to hate with love and of maintaining an optimistic belief in the inevitable, positive outcome of the movement. In so describing themselves, activists gave back something that white America had taken away—a belief in themselves as capable of becoming free and worthy of being free.

The activists also used their songs to describe the world in which they lived and the people who shared that world. In their choice to describe the South, itself, as the root of many of their problems, as opposed to blaming the people of the South, the activists avoided creating protest rhetoric likely to alienate white observers. Unlike many other protestors, the civil rights activists avoided the denigration of their adversary and, in so doing, managed to communicate in ways likely to bolster their own feelings of worth without threatening others.

In their descriptions of the acts in which they should engage to accomplish their goals, the activists chose to urge emotional and psychological preparation for action supporting the cause—primarily to be prepared to love those who would hate them and to remain committed regardless of the trials faced. Such psychological preparation gave the activists the strength to continue to demonstrate and march and go to jail. Themes of transcendence were strong in the activists' blueprint for action. A large part of what they intended to *do* was to become better people. That act would pave the way for accomplishing their ultimate goal—being free.

Important to an understanding of the power of the freedom songs is the realization that singing, in and of itself, carried symbolic meaning in the civil rights movement. Singing involved many people and involved them in ways that no other form of communication could match. When the activists sang, and engaged in the other forms of direct action that advanced the civil rights movement, they showed themselves and their adversaries the distance they had already come. Their acts became proof supporting their claims regarding the creation a new rhetorical being.

Given the present discussion of the freedom songs, one might think that the civil rights movement ended with the joyful embracing of blacks and whites. We know, of course, that the years written of here were followed by years when violence became the province of both blacks and whites, when dreams of "black and white together" were not only forsaken, but repudiated, and when the voices of the singers were silenced in favor of voices advocating a more confrontational, less forgiving engagement with the white power structure. Did activists in the continuing struggle replace the definition of self described here with a different one? They described themselves as evolving—did they continue to change, until the civil rights persona seemed as alien to them as did the hated "Uncle Tom" persona of earlier years? Only continued study of black rhetoric after the civil rights era will shed light on this issue.

In the middle of the 1960s, the singing of freedom songs grew fainter as activists began to sing parodies of the old songs ("too much love, too much love, nothing kills the movement like too much love") and to write new ones expressing the changing mood ("Burn, Baby, Burn").[33] The struggle for black rights moved into the ghettos of major cities and away from nonviolence to "black power," and the rhetoric of the movement changed as well.

Many of the issues raised in the 1960s and the underlying tensions between black and white remain unresolved in the United States of the 1990s. On college campuses and in communities, people struggle for openmindedness and an appreciation of cultural diversity, yet crimes of hate fill the news and white supremacists are elected to public office with rhetoric designed to exploit racial fears in the South. From our contemporary perspective, it may seem naive to have ever thought that the singing of folk songs could make a real difference in such a complex, longstanding problem. Yet, in the face of evidence suggesting that singing holds limited power and that the messages of folksingers reach few ears, people continue to turn to song to address issues of great importance.

The torch of protest singing continues to be carried by many singers who lent their support to civil rights. Matt Jones, a topical song writer active in the civil rights movement, continues to sing "I Love Everybody." Living and singing in New York, he has added the verses:

Hate and greed can't stop it . . .

Racism can't stop it . . .

Howard Beach can't stop it . . .

The CIA can't stop it . . .

I love everybody in my heart.[34]

Peter, Paul, and Mary, in the years after their performance at the March on Washington, split up, got together again, and sang with passion in support of blacks in South Africa. Harry Belafonte, a committed supporter of the civil rights movement, continues to perform, and often introduces audiences of all colors to singers of traditional African music and singers who are adapting such music to popular music form. Guy and Candie Carawan carry on their work at Highlander Research and Education Center in Tennessee and continue to perform their folk music. Pete Seeger, now in his seventies, continues to sing topical songs on many subjects and includes freedom songs in his current repertoire. Topical singer Tom Paxton, who in the 1960s sang of the deaths of "Goodman and Schwerner and Chaney," now sings of the death of Stephen Biko, borrowing a song written by Bernice Johnson Reagon, civil rights songleader and Freedom Singer. Reagon actively continues to advance black causes, both in her role as director of the Program in Black American Culture at the Smithsonian Institution and as the head of the black music group "Sweet Honey in the Rock."

Protest singing is carried forth by a younger generation as well. Young folk singers have gained enormous popularity with songs about oppression and disillusionment and hope. Singing continues to appeal to young African-Americans as it did to earlier activists. In early 1987, for example, students in the Black Caucus at The Pennsylvania State University occupied the telecommunication building on campus for several hours in hopes of drawing administrative attention to their concerns. Before their arrests, the students passed the time by singing. They sang what they knew, "Lean On Me" and "We Are the World," and eventually someone suggested "We Shall Overcome." At first, the others refused to sing the song because, to them, it evoked memories of what they thought of, in part, as the "failure" of the civil rights movement. Twenty-five years after the civil rights activists first argued over the appropriateness of singing the old songs, with reminders of the bad old days of slavery and oppression, the spiritual heirs of that movement reenacted, on a small scale, the debate. In both cases, the old songs were eventually pressed into service but only, in both cases, when the new protestors had made their mark on the songs.[35]

After much discussion, "We Shall Overcome" was sung at Penn State but only with agreed upon changes. The students changed the word "shall" back to "will," as it had been for years before Pete Seeger had introduced the change to "shall." And they changed the reference to "someday" ("we shall overcome someday") to "*today*," because the word "someday" seemed too patient and gradualist for their tastes. The songs, as always, belonged to black tradition, but they also became the property of a new group of singers, protesting in a different time and place, but continuing to achieve the goals sought by generations of African Americans who came before them.

In a world of increasing complexity, in which many people feel overwhelmed and have become cynical, we must welcome the protest singers. They continue to believe that the average person can make a difference, that song really can soothe the savage breast, that singers are teachers and preachers and able to open eyes. Theirs is ultimately a commitment to communication as a alternative to force, to a conviction that, if people will express their hopes and dreams, and listen, and strive to understand, the world can be a better place and that we all can be better people.

NOTES

1. Karen Lebacqz, *Professional Ethics* (Nashville: Abingdon, 1985), 77-91.

2. From "Which Side Are You On?"

3. From "Keep Your Eyes on the Prize" and "Michael Row the Boat Ashore."

4. From "Come By Here" and "Keep Your Eyes on the Prize."

5. From "Do What the Spirit Say Do," "I Love Everybody," and "Hallelujah, I'm A-Traveling."

6. From "We Shall Overcome," "I Love Everybody," "Come By Here," and "I Love Everybody."

7. First two examples from "Come By Here." Third example from "Michael Row the Boat Ashore."

8. From "Over My Head I See Freedom in the Air" and "This Little Light of Mine."

9. From "Which Side Are You On?"

10. From "Hallelujah, I'm A-Traveling," "I'm On My Way to Freedom Land," and "Jacob's Ladder."

11. W. Edson Richmond, "The American Lyric Tradition," in *Our Living Traditions: An Introduction to American Folklore*, ed. Tristram P. Coffin (New York: Basic, 1968), 95.

12. Roger Abrahams and George Foss, *Anglo-American Folksong Style* (Englewood Cliffs: Prentice-Hall, 1968), 87.

13. Abrahams and Foss, *Anglo-American Folksong*, 37.

14. Abrahams and Foss, *Anglo-American Folksong*, 49, 57.

15. Carroll Arnold, *Criticism of Oral Rhetoric* (Columbus, OH: Merrill, 1974), 144.

16. David King Dunaway, *How Can I Keep From Singing?: Pete Seeger* (New York: Da Capo, 1981), 236.

17. From "Ain't Gonna Let Nobody Turn Me 'Round" and "Hallelujah, I'm A-Traveling."

18. From "Michael Row the Boat Ashore."

19. Roderick P. Hart, *Modern Rhetorical Criticism* (Glenview, IL: Scott, Foresman, 1990), 351.

20. Guy Carawan and Candie Carawan, *We Shall Overcome!: Songs of the Southern Freedom Movement* (New York: Oak, 1963), 8; Carawan and Carawan, *We Shall Overcome*, 8; Esau Jenkins in Guy Carawan and Candie Carawan, *Freedom Is a Constant Struggle: Songs of the Freedom Movement* (New York: Oak, 1968), 135; Julius Lester

in Bernice Johnson Reagon, "Songs of the Civil Rights Movement 1955-1965: A Study in Culture History" (Ph.D. diss., Howard University, Washington, D.C., 1975), 161; Reagon, "Songs of the Civil Rights Movement," 132; Bernice Johnson Reagon, booklet accompanying three phonodiscs, *Voices of the Civil Rights Movement: Black American Freedom Songs, 1960-1966* (Washington: Smithsonian Institution, Program in Black American Culture, 1980), 6.

21. Willie Peacock in Pete Seeger and Bob Reiser, *Everybody Says Freedom* (New York: W.W. Norton, 1989), 180; Jane Stembridge in Seeger and Reiser, *Everybody Says*, 36.

22. Hollis Watkins in Seeger and Reiser, *Everybody Says*, 179-180.

23. Hollis Watkins in Seeger and Reiser, *Everybody Says*, 181.

24. Reagon, "Songs of the Civil Rights Movement," 96, 176.

25. Dorothy Cotton in Carawan and Carawan, *Freedom*, 24, 27.

26. Unidentified boy in Seeger and Reiser, *Everybody Says*, 190.

27. Bob Zellner in Carawan and Carawan, *We Shall Overcome*, 21.

28. Julius Lester, "Freedom Songs in the South." *Broadside* 39 (Feb. 7, 1964): 1.

29. Wayne Hampton, *Guerilla Minstrels* (Knoxville: University of Tennessee Press, 1986) 56.

30. Ralph H. Turner, "Determinants of Social Movement Strategies" in *Human Nature and Collective Behavior*, ed. Tamotsu Shibutani (Englewood Cliffs, NJ: Prentice-Hall, 1970), 158.

31. Charles U. Larson, *Persuasion: Reception and Responsibility* (Belmont, CA: Wadsworth, 1989), 173.

32. Karlyn Kohrs Campbell and Kathleen Hall Jamieson, eds., *Form and Genre: Shaping Rhetorical Action* (Falls Church: Speech Communication Association, 1978), 9.

33. Julius Lester in Carawan and Carawan, *Freedom*, 9.

34. Seeger and Reiser, *Everybody Says*, 37.

35. This information was gathered from interviews with students who took part in the demonstration at Penn State.

Appendix

SONG TEXTS AND BACKGROUND

I'll Be All Right

Much has been written about the history of the song that eventually became "We Shall Overcome." According to Bernice Reagon, the song began as a standard traditional black Baptist and Methodist song.[1] She said that "I'll Be All Right" was widely sung around the turn of the century, about the same time that Charles Albert Tindley, a Black Methodist minister wrote a song, "I'll Overcome Someday," with similar words.[2] This song had no musical relationship to the traditional version, in that it was more complicated and formal. According to Reagon, "the isolation of 'I'll overcome' was based on a line from the scriptures, 'ye shall overcome if ye faint not.'"[3] Dunson noted, as did Reagon, that "I'll Be All Right" continued to be sung in the South, even when "We Shall Overcome" was the recognized anthem of the civil rights movement.[4]

I'll be all right,
Well I'll be all right,
Well I'll be all right some day,
All of my troubles will be over
And I'll be free at last.
Well, I'll be all right some day.

I'll be all right,
I'll be all right,
I'll be all right some day.
If in my heart, I do not yield,
I'll be all right some day.

I'll sing my song . . .

I'll overcome . . .

I'll fly away . . .

I'm going home . . .

A slightly different version:[5]

I'll be all right,
I'll be all right,
I'll be all right some day.
If in my heart, I do not yield,
I will be all right some day.

I'll be all right,
I'll be all right,
I'll be all right some day.
All of my troubles will be over,
And I'll be free at last,
Well, I'll be all right some day.

I'm working to be all right . . .

I'm singing to be all right . . .

I'm struggling to be all right . . .

We Shall Overcome (civil rights version)

Musical and Lyrical adaptation by Zilphia Horton, Frank Hamilton, Guy Carawan & Pete Seeger. Inspired by African American Gospel Singing, members of the Food & Tobacco Workers Union, Charleston, S.C., and the southern Civil Rights Movement.

TRO—© Copyright 1960 (renewed 1988) and 1963 (renewed 1991) Ludlow Music, Inc., New York, NY. Used by permission. Royalties derived from this composition are being contributed to the We Shall Overcome Fund and The Freedom Movement under the Trusteeship of the writers.

The songs "I'll Be All Right" and "I'll Overcome Someday" were gradually changed in the oral tradition. "I Will Overcome" was sung as part of the effort to organize the Food, Tobacco and Agricultural Workers Union, in Charleston, South Carolina, in the 1940s, where observers noted that the song seemed to be sung more by black workers than white ones. Zilphia Horton, the music director at Highlander Folk Center in Tennessee, learned the song from workers on the picket lines in Charleston.[6] Pete Seeger learned the song from Zilphia Horton in 1946, and he was responsible for changing the words "we will" to "we shall." Seeger, in turn, taught the song to Guy Carawan in 1950.[7] During the 1950s, "We Shall Overcome" was sung at progressive gatherings in New York and on the West Coast, but it was introduced to the civil rights movement by Carawan when he became music director at Highlander following the death of Zilphia Horton.[8] Carawan taught "We Shall Overcome" to student leaders in 1960, after which it was sung at the founding convention of SNCC in Raleigh, North Carolina.[9]

During the course of the civil rights movement, the singing of "We Shall Overcome" took on a ritualistic nature, with formalized actions accompanying the words. Bernice Reagon remembered Cordell Reagon's efforts "to teach the students the 'proper way' to sing the song that was by then recognized as the theme song of the Movement. It was to be sung at the end of the meeting. While singing the students were told to always stand and link hands, right over left."[10] Reagon went on to comment on the effect of this formalization:

And as a ritual, "We Shall Overcome" was now functioning on a new level. "We Shall Overcome" was not "I'll Be All Right" of the Black church or "We Will Overcome" of the Charleston strike or "We Shall Overcome" in the hands of Peter Seeger and Guy Carawan. It was "We Shall Overcome," the theme song of the Civil Rights Movement. This new identity did not wipe out older identities, nor the early history; however, its strength came not from these earlier efforts but from the power and energy of the Movement of which it was now an integral part.[11]

Reagon's comments suggest that, for African Americans, "We Shall Overcome" served many purposes and that it was often adapted for changing situations.

We shall overcome, we shall overcome,
We shall overcome someday.
Oh-oh, deep in my heart,
I do believe
We shall overcome someday!

We are not afraid, we are not afraid,
We are not afraid today,
Oh deep in my heart, I do believe,
We shall overcome someday.

We shall stand together . . .   Black and white together . . .

The truth will make us free . . .   We shall all be free . . .

The Lord will see us through . . .

We shall live in peace . . .

The whole wide world around . . .

We are not alone . . .

We'll walk hand in hand . . .

I Shall Not Be Moved[12]

As "I Shall Not be Moved," this song was considered a black religious song, a version of which was recorded by Blind Roosevelt Graves in 1929.[13]

I shall not, I shall not be moved,
I shall not, I shall not be moved,
Just like a tree that's planted by the water,
I shall not be moved.

On my way to heaven . . .

Fightin' sinnin' Satan . . .

Jesus is my captain . . .

We Shall Not Be Moved[14]

"We Shall Not Be Moved" was used to encourage black workers to unionize during the 1930s and 1940s.[15] Hille called the song origin a "Negro spiritual" and described this version as "a song that came out of the heart of the South, and spread throughout the country."[16]

We shall not, We shall not be moved;
We shall not, We shall not be moved,
Just like a tree that's standing by the water,
We shall not be moved.

We're fighting for our freedom . . .

Black and white together . . .

Our union is behind us . . .

_____ is our leader . . .

We Shall Not Be Moved[17]

A similar union version was collected by George Korson in 1940.

We shall not, we shall not be moved,
We shall not, we shall not be moved.
Jus' like a tree dat's planted by de water,
We shall not be moved.

John L. Lewis is our leader,
We shall not be moved,
John L. Lewis is our leader,
We shall not be moved.
Jus' like a tree dat's planted by de water,
We shall not be moved.

Mitch is our district president . . .

You can tell de henchmen . . .

Run an' tell de super'tendent . . .

We Shall Not Be Moved (civil rights version)

Adaptation of traditional song. Reprinted from *Sing for Freedom*. ©
1963, 1990 Sing Out Corporation. Used by permission.

We shall not, we shall not be moved,
We shall not, we shall not be moved,
Just like a tree, planted by the water,
We shall not be moved.

We are fighting for our freedom,
We shall not be moved,
We are fighting for our freedom,
We shall not be moved,
Just like a tree, planted by the water,
We shall not be moved.

We are black and white together,
We shall not be moved . . .

We will stand and fight together,
We shall not be moved . . .

The government is behind us,
We shall not be moved . . .

Our parks are integrating,
We shall not be moved . . .

We're sunning on the beaches,
We shall not be moved . . .

Which Side Are You On?[18]

This song is attributed to Florence Reece. She wrote it as a union song in 1931, during the coal miners' strike in Harlan County, Kentucky.[19]

Come all of you good workers,
Good news to you I'll tell,
Of how the good old union has come in here to dwell.

CHORUS
Which side are you on? Which side are you on?
Which side are you on? Which side are you on?

Don't scab for the bosses, don't listen to their lies.
Us poor folks haven't got a chance, unless we organize.

They say in Harlan County, there are no neutrals there.
You'll either be a union man, or a thug for J. H. Blair.

Oh, workers, can you stand it? Oh, tell me how you can.
Will you be a lousy scab, or will you be a man?

My daddy was a miner, and I'm a miner's son,
And I'll stick with the union, till every battle's won.

Which Side Are You On? (civil rights version)

The civil rights version was written by James Farmer. He remembered:

> I rewrote the old labor song by Florence Reece "Which Side Are You On?" on the spur of the moment in the Hinds County Jail, after the Freedom Riders who were imprisoned there had been discussing and speculating about the attitude of local Negroes regarding the Freedom Rides. We had learned through the trustees in the jail that most local Negroes were with us, but afraid to do anything because of fear of reprisals. They told us that, of course, there were a lot of Uncle Toms around and it was hard to tell who was and who was not.[20]

Come all you freedom lovers and listen while I tell,
Of how the freedom riders came to Jackson to dwell.

CHORUS

(Tell me now) Which side are you on,
(Oh won't you tell me) Which side are you on?
(Sing it over now) Which side are you on,
(Once more now) Which side are you on?

My daddy was a freedom rider and I'm a freedom son,
I'll stick right with this struggle until the battle's won.

Don't Tom for Uncle Charlie, don't listen to his lies,
'Cause black folks haven't got a chance until we organize.

They say that in Hinds County, no neutrals have they met,
You're either for the freedom rides or a Tom for Ross Barnett.

Oh people can you stand it, oh tell me how you can,
Will you be an Uncle Tom or will you be a man.

Which Side Are You On?[21]

Len Chandler updated the words later in the civil rights movement, changing the tone of the song significantly.[22]

Come all you bourgeois black men
With all your excess fat
A few days in the county jail
Will sure take care of that.

CHORUS
Oh, which side are you on, boys,
Which side are you on?
Which side are you on, boys,
Which side are you on?

Come all you northern liberals
Take a Klansman out to lunch
But when you dine, instead of wine
You should serve non-violent punch.

Come all you rough, tough bullies
Forget your knives and guns
Non-violence is the only way
The battle can be won.

Come all you high-toned college grads
Pronounce your final 'g's'
But don't you forget your grandma,
She's still scrubbin' on her knees.

Come all you Uncle Toms
Take that hankie from your head
Forget your fears and shed a tear
For the life of shame you've led.

You need not stand our picket lines
If you can't stand the blows
But join your dimes with dollars
Or be counted with our foes.

I heard that Gov. Wallace
Just up and lost his mind
And he bought a case of Man Tan
And joined the picket line.

They say the Ku Klux Klan
Just up and dyes their sheets
And now they sing "Oh Freedom"
Every time they meet.

I've been walkin' so long
I've put blisters on the street
I've caught the freedom fever
And it's settled in my feet.

Don't You Let Nobody Turn You Roun'[23]

Both Bernice Reagon and Arnold Perris reported that the movement song "Ain't Gonna Let Nobody Turn Me Around" had been adapted from an older spiritual. Writers about the civil rights movement used the term "spiritual" loosely, it seems, to mean any song that had been sung in earlier years in a religious context. In the stricter sense of the word, a spiritual was a song sung by Negro slaves prior to the Emancipation Proclamation and the Civil War. There is no evidence that this song was a spiritual in that sense, only that it had been sung in black churches and were a part of that oral tradition. This is an early version of the song that was adopted by civil rights activists.[24]

Don't you let nobody turn you 'roun',
Turn you 'roun'
Don't you let nobody turn you 'roun',
Keep the straight an' the narrow way.

'Twas at the river of Jordan,
Baptism was begun,
John baptized the multitude,
But he sprinkled nary one.

The baptis' they go by water,
The methodes' go by land,
But when they get to heaven,
They'll shake each other's han'.

You may be a good baptis'
An' a good methodes' as well,
But if you ain't the pure in heart
Yo' soul is boun' for hell.

Ain't Gonna Let Nobody Turn Me 'Round
(civil rights version)

Adaptation of traditional song by members of the Albany Movement. Reprinted from *Sing for Freedom.* © 1963, 1990 Sing Out Corporation. Used by permission.

According to Reagon, "Ain't Gonna Let Nobody Turn Me 'Round" was one of the "most powerful statements of the Albany Movement" in 1962 and was sung often in campaigns after Albany. It was sung in response to a federal injunction against demonstrating.[25]

Ain't gonna let nobody, Lordy, turn me 'round,
Turn me 'round, turn me 'round,
Ain't gonna let nobody, Lordy, turn me 'round,
I'm gonna keep on a-walkin, Lord, keep on a-talkin', Lord,
Marching up to freedom land.

Ain't gonna let Nervous Nelly turn me 'round . . .
(term applied to typical segregationist)

Ain't gonna let Chief Pritchett . . .

Ain't gonna let Mayor Kelley . . .

Ain't gonna let segregation . . .

Ain't gonna let Z.T. . . .
(Z.T. Mathews, sheriff of Terrell County, Georgia)

Ain't gonna let no Uncle Tom . . .

Ain't gonna let no fire hose . . .

Ain't gonna let no jailhouse . . .

Ain't gonna let no police dogs . . .

Ain't gonna let no injunction . . .

Rocking Jerusalem[26]

According to Daniel J. Gonczy, the civil rights song "Oh Pritchett, Oh Kelley" was based on a traditional spiritual titled "Rocking Jerusalem."[27]

O Mary O Martha O Mary ring dem bells.
I hear arch angels a-rockin' Jerusalem,
I hear arch angels a-ringin' dem bells.

Church gettin' higher!
Rockin' Jerusalem!
Church gettin' higher!
Ring-a dem bells.

Listen to the lambs . . .

New Jerusalem . . .

Oh Pritchett, Oh Kelley (civil rights version)

Music traditional, words by Bertha Gober and Janie Culbreath. Reprinted from *Sing for Freedom*. © 1963, 1990 Sing Out Corporation. Used by permission.

The civil rights version of this song was adapted by Janie Culbreath and Bertha Gober while they were in the Dougherty County Jail in Georgia. They addressed it to Chief of Police Laurie Pritchett and Mayor Asa D. Kelley of Albany, Georgia.[28]

Oh, Pritchett, Oh, Kelley,
Oh, Pritchett, open them cells.
Oh, Pritchett, Oh, Kelley,
Oh, Pritchett, open them cells.

I hear God's children cryin' for mercy
I hear God's children, prayin' in jail.

I hear God's children you know they're suff'rin',
I hear God's children, prayin' in jail.

Bail's gettin' higher, bail's gettin' higher,
Bail's gettin' higher, bail's gettin' higher,

I hear God's children cryin' for mercy
I hear God's children, prayin' in jail.

I hear God's children you know they're suff'rin',
I hear God's children, prayin' in jail.

Bond's gettin' higher, bond's gettin' higher,
Bond's gettin' higher, bond's gettin' higher,

I hear God's children cryin' for mercy
I hear God's children, prayin' in jail.

I hear God's children you know they're suff'rin',
I hear God's children, prayin' in jail.

Oh Freedom[29]

"Oh Freedom" is another song often referred to as a spiritual by civil rights activists. It is unlikely that any slave would have been so foolish as to express such a blatant desire for freedom, and risk the repercussions, but William Barton's inclusion of this song in his 1899 article does suggest that the song was sung soon after Emancipation.

REFRAIN
Before I'd be a slave, I'd be buried in my grave,
And go home to my Lord and be saved.

O what preaching! O what preaching!
O what preaching over me!

O what mourning! O what mourning!
O what mourning over me!

O what singing . . .

O what shouting . . .

O weeping Mary . . .

O doubting Thomas . . .

O what sighing . . .

Oh, Freedom[30]

Gravlee and Reagon both documented the singing of versions of "Oh Freedom" by blacks protesting the Atlanta race riots of 1906 and later by the Southern Tenant Farmers' Union in the 1930s.[31] This version of the song, and the following two, are those sung by union organizers.

Oh, freedom! oh, freedom!
Oh, freedom over me!
An' befo' I'd be a slave,
I'll be buried in my grave,
An' go home to my Lord an' be free.

No mo' moanin', no mo' moanin',
No mo' moanin' over me!
An befo' I'd be a slave,
I'll be buried in my grave,
An' go home to my Lord an' be free.

No mo' weepin' over me, . . .

There'll be singin' over me, . . .

There'll be shoutin' over me, . . .

There'll be prayin' over me, . . .

Oh, Freedom[32]

Oh freedom, (freedom) Oh freedom (freedom)
Oh freedom over me, (over me)
And before I'd be a slave,
I'll be buried in my grave,
And go home to my Lord and be free (and be free)

No more moaning . . .

No more weeping . . .

No more Jim-crow . . .

There'll be singing . . .

Hille referred to this as "another version that has come into great popularity."[33]

No more mourning, no more mourning,
No more mourning after awhile.
And before I'll be a slave, I'll be buried in my grave;
Take my place with those who loved and fought before.

No more misery . . .

No more starving . . .

No more weeping . . .

I know you're gonna miss me . . .

Oh Freedom (civil rights version)

Oh Freedom Oh Freedom
Oh Freedom over me over me,
And before I'll be a slave
I'll be buried in my grave,
And go home to my Lord and be free.

And there'll be
No segregation, no segregation,
No segregation over me.
And before I'll be a slave,
I'll be buried in my grave
And go home to my Lord and be free.

No more weeping . . .

No more shooting . . .

No burning churches . . .

No more jail houses . . .

No more Jim Crow . . .

No more Barnett . . .

No more Pritchett . . .

Over My Head (civil rights version)

Traditional (African-American Spiritual). Adapted by Bernice Johnson Reagon. Reprinted from *Sing for Freedom*. © 1963, 1990 Sing Out Corporation. Used by permission.

"Over My Head" (or "over My Head I See Freedom in the Air") was derived from earlier songs—"Over My Head I See Trouble in the Air" and "Over My Head I See Music in the Air." Bernice Reagon is credited with introducing the new words that became associated with the civil rights movement, while taking part in the first demonstration in Albany, Georgia, in 1961.[34]

Over my head I see freedom in the air,
Over my head, oh Lord,
I see freedom in the air,
Over my head, I see freedom in the air
There must be a God somewhere.

Over my head I see glory in the air . . .

Over my head there is singing in the air . . .

Over my head I hear praying in the air . . .

Over my head I see victory in the air . . .

Up Above My Head[35]

Adaptation of gospel song by Betty Mae Fikes. Reprinted from *Sing for Freedom*. © 1968, 1990 Sing Out Corporation. Used by permission.

Reagon's song was also adapted later in the movement. The following is an "upbeat gospel version" of the song, developed by Betty Mae Fikes of Selma, Alabama, and introduced at a Sing for Freedom Conference in Atlanta in 1964.[36]

Lead	Group
Up above my head	Up above my head
I see freedom in the air	I see freedom in the air
Up above my head	Up above my head
I see freedom in the air	I see freedom in the air
Up above my head	Up above my head
I see freedom in the air	I see freedom in the air

And I really do believe, I said I really do believe,
    There's a God somewhere.

Up above my head, I hear praying in the air . . .

Up above my head, I hear singing in the air . . .

Up above my head, I hear music in the air . . .

If my mother won't go, I'm gonna go anyhow . . .

If you can't go, let your children go . . .

If my brother can't go, don't let him hinder me . . .

Up above my head, I see freedom in the air . . .

Woke Up This Morning With My Mind On Freedom[37]

According to civil rights activists, this song was derived from one they knew as "Woke Up This Morning With My Mind on Jesus." Bob Zellner remembered that "Reverend Osby of Aurora, Illinois, made up this revamp of an old gospel song ('I woke up this morning with my mind stayed on Jesus') in the Hinds County Jail during the Freedom Rides."[38] The following song fragment, collected in 1919 by Newman I. White, seems to be an antecedent of the civil rights song:

Oh, it ain't no harm to trust in Jesus,
Oh, it ain't no harm to trust in Jesus,
Oh, it ain't no harm to trust in Jesus,
Get on board, get on board.[39]

Woke Up This Morning With My Mind On Freedom
(civil rights version)

Music adapted with additional lyrics by Robert Zellner. © Copyright 1963 (renewed) by FALL RIVER MUSIC. All rights reserved. Used by permission.

Woke up this morning with my mind
(My mind it was) Stayed on freedom,
(Oh yes I) Woke up this morning with my mind
Stayed on freedom,
(Well I) Woke up this morning with my mind
(My mind it was) Stayed on freedom,
Hallelu, hallelu, hallelu, hallelu,
Hallelujah!

Ain't no harm in keep'n' your mind
In keeping it stayed on freedom,
Ain't no harm keep'n' your mind
In keeping it stayed on freedom,
Ain't no harm in keep'n' your mind
In keeping it stayed on freedom,
Hallelu, hallelu, hallelu, hallelu,
Hallelujah!

Walkin' and talkin' with my mind
My mind it was stayed on freedom . . .

Interlude:
You got to walk walk,
You got to walk walk,
You got to walk with your mind on freedom,
You got to talk talk,
You got to talk talk,
You got to talk with your mind on freedom,
Oh oh oh you got to walk walk, talk talk.

Singin' and prayin' with my mind
My mind it was stayed on freedom . . .

Doin' the twist with my mind
My mind it was stayed on freedom . . .

Keep Yore Hand Upon the Chariot[40]

The song that was sung in the civil rights movement as "Keep Your Eyes on the Prize" had a long history prior to the 1960s. These versions are from the early 1900s.

Oh, you better run, oh, you better run,
Oh, you better run, 'fore the train done gone!
Oh, and keep yore hand upon the chariot,
An' yore eyes upon the prize!

For the preacher's comin' an' he preach so bold,
For he preach salvation from out of his soul.
Oh, keep yore hand upon the chariot,
An' yore eyes upon the prize!

Keep Yo' Hand on the Gospel Plow[41]

Keep yo' hand on the gospel plow,
Wouldn't take nothin' for my journey now, Holy Ghost.

CHORUS
Keep yo' hand on the gospel plow,
Hold on, hold on,
Keep your hand on the gospel plow,
Hold on.

Didn't come here for to stay always,
Just come here to fill my place.

I got a mother in the promised land,
Never shall I rest till I shake her hand.

Hold On[42]

Although Cecil Sharp included this version of "Keep Your Eyes on the Prize" in his book on English folksongs, it is closely related to the Negro songs collected earlier by Scarborough and White. Sung by blacks and whites, the song seems to have roots in black oral tradition.

Some of these days about four o'clock,
This old world's going to reel and rock.
Keep your hand,
Keep your hand to the plough, hold on.

CHORUS
Hold on, hold on,
Keep your hand,
Keep your hand to the plough, hold on.

Some of these days, but I don't know when,
This old world's going to end.
Keep your hand to the plough, hold on.

Go away, Satan, let me be,
You fooled my brother, but you can't fool me.

Satan wears a sinful shoe,
If you don't mind he'll slip it on you.

Some of these mornings at the rising sun,
O God's going to stop your lying tongue.

Hain't been to heaven, but I've been told
That the streets are pearl and the gates are gold.

When I get to heaven I'm going to sit down,
Wear a white robe and a starry crown.

I'm going to heaven and I hain't going to stop,
There hain't going to be no stumbling-block.

Keep Your Hand on the Plow[43]

Versions of "Keep Your Eyes on the Prize" continued to be represented in the oral tradition throughout the 1900s. The versions collected by the Lomaxes include references to the biblical story of Paul and Silas, which was retained by civil rights activists, and verses adapted to celebrate the end of World War II.

Mary wo' three links of chain,
Ev'ry link was Jesus' name.
Keep your hand on the plow,
Hold on.

CHORUS
Hold on, hold on,
Keep your hand on the plow,
Hold on.

Paul and Silas bound in jail,
Had nobody for to go their bail,
Keep your hand on the plow,
Hold on.

Paul and Silas began to shout,
Jail doors opened and they walked out. . .

Peter was so nice and neat,
Wouldn't let Jesus wash his feet . . .

Jesus said, "If I wash them not,
You'll have no father in this lot" . . .

Peter got anxious and he said,
"Wash my feet, my hands and head," . . .

Got my hand on the gospel plow,
Wouldn't take nothin' for my journey now, . . .

Version II

United Nations make a chain,
Every link is freedom's name, . . .

Now the war is over and done
Let's keep the peace that we have won, . . .

Freedom's name is mighty sweet,
All this world is gonna meet, . . .

Many men have fought and died
So we could sing here side by side, . . .

Keep Your Eyes On the Prize (civil rights version)

The activists for civil rights reintroduced the word change from "keep your hand on the plow" to "keep your eyes on the prize," in fact believing that it originated with them.[44] The song became very popular in the civil rights movement, partly because it "had meaning for the sit-in students who were the first to be 'bound in jail' for long periods of time. It went with the Freedom Riders to Jackson and into Parchman, and then on to Albany and all of the many other areas of struggle."[45]

Paul and Silas, bound in jail,
Had no money for to go their bail,
Keep your eyes on the prize, hold on, hold on.

CHORUS
Hold on, hold on,
Keep your eyes on the prize,
Hold on, hold on.

Paul and Silas begin to shout,
The jail door opened and they walked out,
Keep your eyes on the prize, hold on.

Freedom's name is mighty sweet,
Black and white are gonna meet.

Got my hand on the Gospel plow,
I wouldn't take nothin' for my journey now.

The only chain that a man can stand,
Is that chain of hand in hand.

The only that we did wrong,
Stayed in the wilderness a day too long.

But the one thing we did right,
Was the day we started to fight.

We're gonna board that big Greyhound,
Carryin' love from town to town.

We're gonna ride for civil rights,
We're gonna ride both black and white.

We've met jail and violence too,
But God's love has seen us through.

Haven't been to heaven but I've been told,
Streets up there are paved with gold.

Albenny Georgia lives in race
We're goin' to fight it from place to place

I know what I think is right
Freedom in the souls of black and white

Singing and shouting is very well
Get off your seat and go to jail

Jordan River is deep and wide
We'll find freedom on the other side.

Unnamed version of
I'm Gonna Sit at the Welcome Table[46]

The song that became known as "I'm Gonna Sit at the Welcome Table" during the civil rights movement seems to have been a compilation of stock verses from several sources. The following song, for instance, was collected in 1919 and includes two verses very similar to those in the civil rights version.

I'm gwine to tell my loving Saviour,
I'm gwine to tell my loving Saviour,
Some of these days, God knows.

I'm gwine to tell him all my troubles . . .

I'm gwine to eat at the welcome table . . .

I'm gwine ride in the golden chariot . . .

I'm gwine whip the golden horses . . .

Christa Dixon included the following verses in versions of "Jacob's Ladder" and "Members, Don't Get Weary":[47]

I'm goin' to set at de welcome table, welcome table
I'm goin' to set at de welcome table, welcome table
I'm goin' to set at de welcome table, welcome table
Save me Jedus save me now.

O, I'm gwine to set at de welcome table, O yes
O, I'm gwine to set at de welcome table, O yes
O, I'm gwine to set at de welcome table, O yes
When my work is done.

The line "I'm going to tell him [Jesus] how you 'buse me" also appeared in White's book, *American Negro Folk Songs*.[48]

I'm Gonna Sit at the Welcome Table
(civil rights version)

© 1960 Alpha Music. Used by permission.

"I'm Gonna Sit at the Welcome Table" was adapted for the civil rights movement at Highlander Folk School and "became a musical statement during the Sit-in Movement."[49]

I'm gonna sit at the welcome table,
I'm gonna sit at the welcome table one of these days
Hallelujah,
I'm gonna sit at the welcome table,
Gonna sit at the welcome table one of these days.

I'm gonna walk the streets of glory,
I'm gonna walk the streets of glory
One of these days, hallelujah,
I'm gonna walk the streets of glory,
I'm gonna walk the streets of glory . . .
One of these days.

I'm gonna tell God how you treated me . . .

I'm gonna get my civil rights . . .

I'm gonna sit at Woolworth's lunch counter . . .

This Little Light of Mine (civil rights version)

Traditional song. Reprinted from *Sing for Freedom*. © 1963, 1990 Sing Out Corporation. Used by permission.

"This Little Light of Mine" was a "traditional gospel song" prior to the civil rights movement, one that Reagon remembered "I'd sung all my life."[50] The activists changed verses and added new ones to adapt the song for their needs.

This-a little light of mine,
I'm gonna let it shine (oh)
This little light of mine,
I'm gonna let it shine, let it shine,
Let it shine, let it shine.

BRIDGE
The light that shines is the light of love,
Lights the darkness from above,
It shines on me and it shines on you,
Shows what the power of love can do,
I'm gonna shine my light both far and near,
I'm gonna shine my light both bright and clear,
Where there's a dark corner in this land,
I'm gonna let my little light shine.

VERSES
We've got the light of freedom,
We're gonna let it shine . . .

Deep down in the South,
We're gonna let it shine . . .

Down in Birmingham (Mississippi, Alabama, etc.),
We're gonna let it shine . . .

Everywhere I go,
I'm gonna let it shine . . .

Tell Chief Pritchett,
I'm gonna let it shine . . .

All in the jail house,
I'm gonna let it shine . . .

BRIDGE
On Monday he gave me the gift of love
Tuesday peace came from above
Wednesday he told me to have more faith
Thursday he gave me a little more grace
Friday he told me just to watch and pray
Saturday told me just what to say
Sunday he gave me the power divine --
To let my little light shine.

It was common, in "This Little Light of Mine," to start with a state
or city name and then broaden the scope or, conversely, shrink it to be
more specific.[51]

All over the state of Georgia . . .
All over the southland . . .
All over America . . .
All over the world now . . .

All over the state of Georgia . . .
All over the city of Atlanta . . .
On this street called Peachtree . . .
Here in this building . . .
Deep in my heart . . .

Other verses were remembered by Dunson:[52]

Up and down this street Lord,   Voting for my Freedom,
I'm going to let it shine . . .   I'm going to let it shine . . .

Every time I'm bleeding,
I'm going to let it shine . . .

Do What the Spirit Say Do (civil rights version)

Adaptation of traditional song by young people in Selma. Reprinted from *Sing for Freedom.* © 1968, 1990 Sing Out Corporation. Used by permission.

"Do What the Spirit Say Do" is another song characterized by activists as a song they had learned through the oral tradition and that they recognized as an older, religious song.

Do what the spirit says do,
We're gonna do what the spirit says do,
What the spirit says do, we're gonna do, oh Lord,
We're gonna do what the spirit says do.

You gotta do what the spirit say do,
You gotta do what the spirit say do,
And what the spirit say do, I'm gonna do, oh Lord,
You gotta do what the spirit say do.

You gotta march . . .	You gotta cool it . . .
You gotta sing . . .	You gotta love . . .
You gotta moan . . .	You gotta die . . .
You gotta picket . . .	
You gotta vote . . .	
You gotta move . . .	
You gotta pray . . .	
You gotta preach . . .	
You gotta shout . . .	
You gotta rock . . .	

(Everybody Says) Freedom (civil rights version)

Adaptation of traditional song by members of SNCC. Reprinted from *Sing for Freedom.* © 1963, 1990 Sing Out Corporation. Used by permission.

This song began its life in the civil rights movement in its original form—during the Montgomery bus boycott in 1955, the activists sang "Amen, amen." The change to "Freedom, freedom" was made during the Nashville sit-ins and the song "became the heart of the Nashville Movement," according to activist John Lewis.[53] The activists also changed other words in the song to reflect their situation and concerns. Sung in the call and response form, the leader's words appear here in parentheses. In some versions, each verse begins "everybody *sing* freedom."

(Everybody says) Freedom
(Everybody says) Freedom
(Everybody says) Freedom, freedom, freedom.

(In the cottonfield) Freedom,
(In the schoolroom) Freedom,
(In the jailhouse) Freedom, freedom, freedom.

(Everybody says) Civil rights . . .

(All across the South) . . .

(In Mississippi) . . .

(In spite of Ross Barnett) . . .

(Gain the victory) . . .

I Love Everybody (civil rights version)

Adaptation of spiritual—SCLC. Reprinted from *Sing for Freedom.* ©
1968, 1990 Sing Out Corporation. Used by permission.

"I Love Everybody" is another song adapted from what activists
called a spiritual; they changed the older song by adding localized
verses.

I love everybody
I love everybody
I love everybody, in my heart.

I love everybody
I love everybody
I love everybody, in my heart.

You can't make me doubt it . . .

The Klan can't make me doubt it . . .

I feel the fire burning . . .

I know freedom is a-comin' . . .

Matt Jones added these verses more recently:[54]

Hate and greed can't stop it . . .

Racism can't stop it . . .

Howard Beach can't stop it . . .

The CIA can't stop it . . .

If You Miss Me at the Back of the Bus

According to Kay Mills, in her biography of Fannie Lou Hamer, this song was sung to the tune of "Oh, Mary."[55]

If you miss me at the back of the bus,
And you can't find me nowhere,
Come on up to the front of the bus,
I'll be ridin' up there.
I'll be ridin' up there, I'll be ridin' up there.
Come on up to the front of the bus, I'll be ridin' up there.

If you miss me at the front of the bus,
And you can't find me nowhere,
Come on up to the driver's seat,
I'll be drivin' up there.
I'll be drivin' up there, I'll be drivin' up there,
Come on up to the driver's seat, I'll be drivin' up there.

If you miss me at Jackson State,
And you can't find me nowhere,
Come on over to Ole Miss, I'll be studyin' over there . . .

If you miss me from knockin' on doors,
And you can't find me nowhere,
Come on down to the registrar's room, I'll be the
registrar there . . .

If you miss me in the cotton field,
And you can't find me nowhere,
Come on down to the courthouse, I'll be voting right there . . .

If you miss me from the picket line,
And you can't find me nowhere,
Come on down to the jail house, I'll be rooming down there . . .

If you miss me in the Mississippi River,
And you can't find me nowhere,
Come on down to the city pool, I'll be swimming in there . . .

Bob Cohen, director of the Mississippi Caravan of Music recalled
additional verses:[56]

If you miss me in the Missus kitchen,
And you can't find me nowhere,
Come on over to Washington
I'll be Congresswoman there. . .

If you miss me in the Freedom fight
And you can't find me nowhere,
Come on over to the graveyard
I'll be buried over there.

I Ain't Scared of Your Jail

Carawan and Carawan record the words of this song as follows:[57]

I ain't scared of your jail, because I want my freedom,
I want my freedom, I want my freedom.
I ain't scared of your jail, because I want my freedom,
I want my freedom, now!

We'll march downtown because, we want our freedom . . .

We'll go to jail because . . .

I served ninety days because . . .

"You know in all parts of the South the use dogs and sic 'em on people, and they use cattle prods. Not only that, but they beat you upside the head with sticks. They squirt water on you with a big hose. So sometimes we sing:"

I ain't scared of your dogs, because . . .

I ain't scared of your sticks, because . . .

I ain't scared of your hose, because . . .

"And sometimes they tell us, 'Well, since you ain't scared of nothin', I'm gonna go back to the old Southern tradition—I'm gonna blow your brains out.' So we sing:"

I don't mind dying because . . .

"And while things are going on in Mississippi, people are doing things in other places. In Birmingham they sing:"

I ain't scared of no Bull [Connor] because . . .

I'm On My Way[58]

This version of "I'm On My Way" was collected by White in 1925. As was typical, the older song stressed a religious theme while the civil rights adaptation emphasized freedom. Other versions make "Canaan land" the destination instead of "the heavenly land."[59]

I'm on my way to the heavenly land,
I'm on my way to the heavenly land,
I'm on my way to the heavenly land,
I'm on my way, God knows I'm on my way.

If the seeker won't go, I'll journey on . . .

If my sister won't go, I'll journey on . . .

I'm On My Way to the Freedom Land
(civil rights version)

Adaptation of traditional song. Reprinted from *Sing for Freedom.* © 1963, 1990 Sing Out Corporation. Used by permission.

I'm on my way to freedom land,
I'm on my way to freedom land,
I'm on my way to freedom land,
I'm on my way, great God, I'm on my way.

I asked my brother to come [and go] with me . . .
I'm on my way, great God, I'm on my way.

If he can't go, I'm gonna go anyhow . . .
I'm on my way, great God, I'm on my way.

If you can't go, don't hinder me . . .
I'm on my way, great God, I'm on my way.

If you can't go, let your children go . . .
I'm on my way, great God, I'm on my way.

Hallelujah, I'm A-Traveling[60]

"Hallelujah, I'm A-Traveling" had a long history as a black protest song before it reached the civil rights movement. It was sung, for instance, as part of a black protest in Columbia, Tennessee, in 1946.

I read in the news the Supreme Court said,
Listen here, Mr. Jim Crow, it's time you was dead.

The judges declared in Washington town,
You white folks must take that old Jim Crow sign down.

Columbia's the gem of the ocean they say,
We're fighting Jim Crow in Columbia today.

Well, I hate Jim Crow and Jim Crow hates me,
That's why I'm fighting for my liberty.

Hallelujah, I'm A-Traveling (civil rights version)

New Words by Harry Raymond.
© Copyright 1947 (renewed) by STORMKING MUSIC INC.
All rights reserved. Used by permission.

Stand up and rejoice, a great day is here.
We're fighting Jim Crow and the vic'try is near.

CHORUS
Hallelujah, I'm a-traveling,
Hallelujah, ain't it fine,
Hallelujah, I'm a-traveling,
Down freedom's main line.

I'm paying my fare on the Greyhound bus line.
I'm riding the front seat to Montgomery this time.

In Nashville, Tennessee, I can order a coke.
The waitress at Woolworth's knows it's no joke.

I walked in Montgomery, I sat in Tennessee,
And now I'm riding for equality.

I'm traveling to Mississippi on the Greyhound bus lines.
Hallelujah, I'm a-riding the front seat this time.

In old Fayette County, set off and remote
The polls are now open for Negroes to vote.

In Nineteen Fifty-four, the Supreme Court has said,
Looka here, Mr. Jim Crow, it's time you were dead.

I Been 'Buked[61]

The freedom song "We'll Never Turn Back" was loosely based on this song, collected in 1915-1916.

I been 'buked and I been 'bused,
I been 'buked and I been 'bused.
I'm gwine ter lay down dis world
An' shoulder up my cross,
An' I'll take it home ter Je-sus,
Ain't dat good news.

We'll Never Turn Back (civil rights version)

Bertha Gober. © Copyright 1964 (Renewed) Chappell & Co. All rights reserved. Used by permission. Warner Bros. Publications U.S. Inc., Miami, FL 33014

We've been 'buked and we've been scorned.
We've been talked about sure's you're born.

CHORUS
But we'll never turn back,
No we'll never turn back,
Until we've all been free and we have equality.

We have walked through the shadows of death.
We've had to walk all by ourself.

We have served our time in jail
With no money for to go our bail.

Double verse
We have hung our heads and cried,
Cried for those like Lee who died,
Died for you and died for me,
Died for the cause of equality.

Come By Here (Kum Ba Yah)
(civil rights version)

"Come By Here" was composed in the 1930s by Reverend Marvin Frey. The song was then taken by missionaries to Angola, where it was changed to "Kum Ba Yah," before being returned to the U.S. The civil rights activists generally sang it as "Come By Here" and added verses to address their goals.[62]

Come by here, my Lordy, come by here.
Come by here, my Lordy, come by here.
Come by here, my Lordy, come by here.
Oh Lord, come by here.

Churches are burning here, come by here . . .

Someone's starving, Lord, come by here . . .

Someone's shooting, Lord, come by here . . .

We want justice, Lord, come by here . . .

We want freedom here, come by here . . .

Michael Row the Boat Ashore[63]

"Michael Row the Boat Ashore" was one of two songs sung by civil rights activists that seems likely to have been sung by Negro slaves as well. A version of the song appears in the 1867 book, *Slave Songs of the United States.*

Michael row de boat ashore, Hallelujah!
Michael row de boat ashore, Hallelujah!

Michael boat a gospel boat, Hallelujah!

I wonder where my mudder deh (there) . . .

See my mudder on de rock gwine home . . .

On de rock gwine home in Jesus' name . . .

Michael boat a music boat . . .

Gabriel blow de trumpet horn . . .

O you mind your boastin' talk . . .

Boastin' talk will sink your soul . . .

Brudder, lend a helpin' hand . . .

Sister, help for trim dat boat . . .

Jordan stream is wide and deep . . .

Jesus stand on t' oder side . . .

I wonder if my maussa deh . . .

My fader gone to unknown land . . .

He raise de fruit for you to eat . . .

He dat eat shall neber die . . .

When de river oberflow . . .

O poor sinner, how you land? . . .

Riber run and darkness comin' . . .

Sinner row to save you soul . . .

Michael Row the Boat Ashore
(civil rights version)

Adapted with additional words by Tony Salatan, Lee Hays, Ronnie Gilbert, & Fred Hellerman. © Copyright 1958, 1962 (renewed) by SANGA MUSIC INC. All rights reserved. Used by permission.

Michael row the boat ashore, Alleluja.
Michael row the boat ashore, Alleluja.

Michael's boat is a freedom boat, Alleluja.
If you stop singing then it can't float, Alleluja.

Jordan's river is deep and wide, Alleluja.
Get my freedom on the other side, Alleluja.

Jordan's river is chilly and cold, Alleluja.
Chills the body but not the soul, Alleluja.

Christian brothers, don't you know, Alleluja.
Mississippi is the next to go, Alleluja.

Jacob's Ladder[64]

"Jacob's Ladder" is a folk song that has been, and continues to be adapted for many protest movements. Sung by blacks as early as the 1860s, it may have been a slave spiritual.

I want to climb up Jacob's ladder,
Jacob's ladder, O Jacob's ladder,
I want to climb up Jacob's ladder,
But I can't climb it till I make my peace with the Lord.

O praise ye the Lord,
I'll praise Him till I die,
I'll praise Him till I die,
And sing Jerusalem.

Jacob's Ladder[65]

Another black version, one of many variants, appeared in Work's *American Negro Songs.*

We are climbing Jacob's ladder,
We are climbing Jacob's ladder,
We are climbing Jacob's ladder,
Soldiers of the Cross.

Every round goes higher 'n' higher . . .

Brother do you love my Jesus . . .

If you love him why not serve him . . .

"Jacob's Ladder" was also adopted by union organizers. West Virginia miners used the tune and sang "We have worked in dark and danger, workers in the mine." It was sung by North Carolina Textile workers as "We are building a strong union, workers in the mill."[66]

Jacob's Ladder (civil rights version)

We are climbing Jacob's ladder.
We are climbing Jacob's ladder.
We are climbing Jacob's ladder,
Brothers, sisters, all.

Every rung goes higher, higher . . .

Every new one makes us stronger . . .

Verses are still being added as this song is adapted for new causes. The women's movement, for example, has adopted the song for their purposes.[67]

We are dancing Sarah's circle . . .
Sisters, brothers, all.

Every round a generation . . .

Struggle's long but hope is longer . . .

People all need jobs and justice . . .

Freedom Is A Constant Struggle

They say that freedom is a constant struggle,
They say that freedom is a constant struggle,
They say that freedom is a constant struggle,
Oh Lord, we've struggled so long,
We must be free, we must be free.

They say that freedom is a constant crying . . .
Oh Lord, we've cried so long . . .

They say that freedom is a constant sorrow . . .
Oh Lord, we've sorrowed so long . . .

They say that freedom is a constant moaning . . .
Oh Lord, we've moaned so long . . .

They say that freedom is a constant dying . . .
Oh Lord, we've died so long . . .

NOTES

1. Bernice Reagon, "Songs of the Civil Rights Movement 1955-1965: A Study in Culture History" (Ph.D. diss., Howard University, 1975), 65.

2. Reagon, "Songs of the Civil Rights Movement," 69.

3. Reagon, "Songs of the Civil Rights Movement," 70.

4. Josh Dunson, *Freedom in the Air: Song Movements of the Sixties* (New York: International, 1965), 102.

5. Guy Carawan and Candie Carawan, *Freedom Is a Constant Struggle: Songs of the Freedom Movement* (New York: Oak, 1968), 139.

6. Reagon, "Songs of the Civil Rights Movement," 70-76.

7. Pete Seeger and Bob Reiser, *Everybody Says Freedom* (New York: W.W. Norton, 1989), 8.

8. Reagon, "Songs of the Civil Rights Movement," 78-80.

9. Seeger and Reiser, *Everybody Says*, 11.

10. Reagon, "Songs of the Civil Rights Movement," 132.

11. Reagon, "Songs of the Civil Rights Movement," 132-133.

12. Bruce Jackson, "The Glory Songs of the Lord," in *Our Living Traditions: An Introduction to American Folklore*, ed. Tristram Potter Coffin (New York: Basic, 1968), 117.

13. Paul Oliver, *Songsters and Saints: Vocal Traditions on Race Records* (Cambridge: Cambridge University Press, 1984), 205.

14. Waldemar Hille, *The People's Song Book* (1948. New York: Oak, 1961), 95.

15. G. Jack Gravlee, "A Black Rhetoric of Social Revolution," in *A New Diversity in Contemporary Southern Rhetoric*, ed. Calvin M. Logue and Howard Dorgan (Baton Rouge: Louisiana State University Press, 1987), 62; Reagon, "Songs of the Civil Rights Movement," 56.

16. Hille, *People's Song Book*, 95.

17. George Korson, *Coal Dust on the Fiddle* (Hatboro, PA: Folklore Associates, 1965), 315.

18. Hille, *People's Song Book*, 92.

19. Gravlee, "Black Rhetoric," 62.

20. Guy Carawan and Candie Carawan, *We Shall Overcome!: Songs of the Southern Freedom Movement* (New York: Oak, 1963), 43.

21. Carawan and Carawan, *Freedom*, 160-161.

22. Carawan and Carawan, *Freedom*, 160-161.

23. John W. Work, *American Negro Songs and Spirituals* (New York: Bonanza, 1940), 89.

24. Reagon, "Songs of the Civil Rights Movement," 138; Arnold Perris, *Music As Propaganda: Art To Persuade, Art To Control* (Westport, CT: Greenwood, 1985), 189.

25. Reagon, "Songs of the Civil Rights Movement," 138.

26. Work, *American Negro Songs*, 226.

27. Daniel J. Gonczy, "The Folk Music Movement of the 1960s: Its Rise and Fall," *Popular Music and Society* 10.1 (1985): 24.

28. Carawan and Carawan, *We Shall Overcome*, 62.

29. William E. Barton, "Hymns of the Slave and Freedman," *New England Magazine* (January 1899), 98.

30. Nathaniel Dett, *Religious Folk Songs of the Negro* (Hampton, VA: Hampton Institute Press, 1927), 110.

31. Gravlee, "Black Rhetoric," 61; Reagon, "Songs of the Civil Rights Movement," 39.

32. Hille, *People's Song Book*, 21.

33. Hille, *People's Song Book*, 21.

34. Reagon, "Songs of the Civil Rights Movement," 134-135; see also Dunson, *Freedom in the Air*, 63, and Carawan and Carawan, *We Shall Overcome*, 75.

35. Carawan and Carawan, *Freedom*, 52-55.

36. Carawan and Carawan, *Freedom*, 52.

37. Carawan and Carawan, *We Shall Overcome*, 81-83; Seeger and Reiser, *Everybody Says*, 175-177.

38. Carawan and Carawan, *We Shall Overcome*, 81.

39. Newman I. White, *American Negro Folk-Songs* (Cambridge: Harvard University Press, 1928), 65.

40. Dorothy Scarborough, *On the Trail of Negro Folk-Songs* (Cambridge: Harvard University Press, 1925), 256.

41. White, *American Negro Folk-Songs*, 115.

42. Cecil Sharp, *English Folk Songs from the Southern Appalachians*, volume 2 (London: Oxford University Press, 1932), 292.

43. John A. Lomax and Alan Lomax, *Folk Song, U.S.A.* (New York: New American Library, 1975), 468-469.

44. Carawan and Carawan attribute the word change to Alice Wine. It is possible that Wine had, at some point, heard sung an early version of the song that, like the one collected by Scarborough in the 1920s, used the words "keep your eyes on the prize."

45. Carawan and Carawan, *We Shall Overcome*, 111.

46. White, *American Negro Folk-Songs*, 120.

47. Christa Dixon, *Negro Spirituals* (Wuppertal: Jugenddienst-Verlag, 1967), 139, 213.

48. White, *American Negro Folk-Songs*, 113. This line appears in the song "Most Done Suffering."

49. Carawan and Carawan, *We Shall Overcome*, 14; Reagon, "Songs of the Civil Rights Movement," 109.

50. Perris, *Music as Propaganda*, 188; Reagon in Juan Williams, *Eyes on the Prize: America's Civil Rights Years, 1954-1965* (New York: Viking, 1987), 177.

51. Seeger and Reiser, *Everybody Says*, 240.

52. Dunson, *Freedom in the Air*, 101.

53. John Lewis in Reagon, "Songs of the Civil Rights Movement," 102.

54. Seeger and Reiser, *Everybody Says*, 37.

55. Kay Mills, *This Little Light of Mine: The Life of Fannie Lou Hamer* (New York: Dutton, 1993), 93.

56. Mills, *Little Light*, 93.

57. Guy Carawan and Candie Carawan, eds. and comps., *Sing for Freedom: The Story of the Civil Rights Movement Through Its Songs* (Bethlehem, PA: Sing Out, 1990), 150.

58. White, *American Negro Folk-Songs*, 118.

59. Seeger and Reiser, *Everybody Says*, 56.

60. Seeger and Reiser, *Everybody Says*, 63.

61. White, *American Negro Folk-Songs*, 75.

62. Seeger and Reiser, *Everybody Says*, 128.

63. William Francis Allen, et al., *Slave Songs of the United States* (1867. New York: Peter Smith, 1951), 23-24.

64. Allen, et al., *Slave Songs*, 97.

65. Work, *American Negro Songs*, 220. See also Dett, *Religious Folk Songs of the Negro*, 118; White, *American Negro Folk-Songs*, 59-60; Dixon, *Negro Spirituals*, 139-141.

66. Seeger and Reiser, *Everybody Says*, 247; see also Robert Sherman, "Sing a Song of Freedom" in *The American Folk Scene: Dimensions of the Folksong Revival*, edited by David A. DeTurk and A. Poulin, Jr. (New York: Dell, 1967), 175.

67. Seeger and Reiser, *Everybody Says*, 250.

Bibliography

Abrahams, Roger, and George Foss. *Anglo-American Folksong Style*. Englewood Cliffs, NJ: Prentice-Hall, 1968.

Allen, William Francis, Charles Pickard Ware, and Lucy McKim Garrison. *Slave Songs of the United States*. 1867. New York: Peter Smith, 1951.

Ames, Russell. *The Story of American Folk Song*. New York: Grosset, 1955.

Aptheker, Herbert. *American Negro Slave Revolts*. 1943. New York: International, 1969.

Arnold, Carroll. *Criticism of Oral Rhetoric*. Columbus, OH: Merrill, 1974.

Barton, William E. "Hymns of the Slave and Freedman." *New England Magazine*, January 1899, 90-103.

"Battle Hymn of the Integrationists." *U.S. News and World Report*, 5 August 1963, 8.

Benson, Thomas W. "Implicit Communication Theory in Campaign Coverage." In *Television Coverage of the 1980 Presidential Campaign*, edited by William C. Adams, 103-116. Norwood, NJ: ABLEX, 1983.

Blumer, Herbert. "Social Movements." In *The Sociology of Dissent*, edited by R. Serge Denisoff, 4-20. New York: Harcourt, 1974.

Branch, Taylor. *Parting the Waters: America in the King Years 1954-63*. New York: Simon and Schuster, 1988.

Burke, Kenneth. *A Grammar of Motives*. Englewood Cliffs, NJ: Prentice-Hall, 1945.

———. *Philosophy of Literary Form*. 3d ed., rev. Berkeley: University of California Press, 1973.

Campbell, Karlyn Kohrs. *Critiques of Contemporary Rhetoric*. Belmont, CA: Wadsworth, 1972.

Campbell, Karlyn Kohrs, and Kathleen Hall Jamieson, eds. *Form and Genre: Shaping Rhetorical Action*. Falls Church, VA: Speech Communication Association, 1978.

Carawan, Guy, and Candie Carawan. *We Shall Overcome!: Songs of the Southern Freedom Movement.* New York: Oak, 1963.

————. *Freedom Is a Constant Struggle: Songs of the Freedom Movement.* New York: Oak, 1968.

————, eds. and comps. *Sing for Freedom: The Story of the Civil Rights Movement Through Its Songs.* Bethlehem, PA: Sing Out, 1990.

Carey, James W. *Communication as Culture: Essays on Media and Society.* Boston: Unwin Hyman, 1989.

Cone, James H. *The Spirituals and the Blues.* New York: Seabury, 1972.

Cotton, Dorothy. Lecture at The Pennsylvania State University, April 4, 1988.

Crowell, Laura. "The Building of the 'Four Freedoms Speech.'" *Speech Monographs* 22 (1955): 266-283.

DeTurk, David A., and A. Poulin, Jr., eds. *The American Folk Scene: Dimensions of the Folksong Revival.* New York: Dell, 1967.

Dett, Nathaniel. *Religious Folk Songs of the Negro.* Hampton, VA: Hampton Institute Press, 1927.

Dixon, Christa. *Negro Spirituals.* Wuppertal: Jugenddienst-Verlag, 1967.

Dunaway, David King. *How Can I Keep From Singing: Pete Seeger.* New York: Da Capo, 1981.

Dunson, Josh. *Freedom in the Air: Song Movements of the Sixties.* New York: International, 1965.

Epstein, Dena J. *Sinful Tunes and Spirituals.* Urbana: University of Illinois Press, 1977.

Farmer, James. *Lay Bare the Heart: An Autobiography of the Civil Rights Movement.* New York: Arbor, 1985.

Fisher, Miles Mark. *Negro Slave Songs.* New York: Atheneum, 1953.

Fox-Genovese, Elizabeth. "Strategies and Forms of Resistance: Focus on Slave Women in the United States." In *In Resistance: Studies in African, Caribbean, and Afro-American History,* edited by Gary Y. Okihiro, 143-65. Amherst: University of Massachusetts Press, 1986.

Francesconi, Robert. "Free Jazz and Black Nationalism: A Rhetoric of Musical Style." *Critical Studies in Mass Communication* 3 (1986): 36-49.

Fredrickson, George M., and Christopher Lasch. "Resistance to Slavery." In *The Debate Over Slavery: Stanley Elkins and His Critics*, edited by Ann J. Lane, 223-44. Urbana: University of Illinois Press, 1971.

Freire, Paulo. *Pedagogy of the Oppressed*. Translated by Myra Bergman Ramos. New York: Continuum, 1984.

Gates, David. "Our Stories, Our Selves." *Newsweek* 23 January 1989, 64.

Gates, Henry Louis, Jr. *The Signifying Monkey: A Theory of African-American Literary Criticism*. New York: Oxford University Press, 1988.

Gitlin, Todd. *The Whole World is Watching: Mass Media in the Making and Unmaking of the New Left*. Berkeley: University of California Press, 1980.

Goffman, Erving. *The Presentation of Self in Everyday Life*. New York: Overlook, 1973.

Goldenberg, I. Ira. *Oppression and Social Intervention*. Chicago: Nelson, 1978.

Gonczy, Daniel J. "The Folk Music Movement of the 1960s: Its Rise and Fall." *Popular Music and Society* 10.1 (1985): 15-31.

Gravlee, G. Jack. "A Black Rhetoric of Social Revolution." In *A New Diversity in Contemporary Southern Rhetoric*, edited by Calvin M. Logue and Howard Dorgan, 52-88. Baton Rouge: Louisiana State University Press, 1987.

Gregg, Richard B. "The Ego-Function of the Rhetoric of Protest." *Philosophy and Rhetoric* 4 (1971): 71-91.

Hampton, Henry, and Steve Fayer. *Voices of Freedom: An Oral History of the Civil Rights Movement from the 1950s through the 1980s*. New York: Bantam, 1990.

Hampton, Wayne. *Guerilla Minstrels*. Knoxville: University of Tennessee Press, 1986.

Hart, Roderick P. *Modern Rhetorical Criticism*. Glenview, IL: Scott, Foresman, 1990.

Hille, Waldemar. *The People's Song Book*. 1948. New York: Oak, 1961.

Hoffer, Eric. *The True Believer*. New York: Harper, 1966.

Irvine, James R., and Walter G. Kirkpatrick. "The Musical Form in Rhetorical Exchange: Theoretical Considerations." *Quarterly Journal of Speech* 58 (1972): 272-284.

Jackson, Bruce. "The Glory Songs of the Lord." In *Our Living Traditions: An Introduction to American Folklore*, edited by Tristram Potter Coffin, 108-119. New York: Basic, 1968.

Johnson, Bonnie M. "Images of the Enemy in Intergroup Conflict." *Central States Speech Journal*, 26 (1975): 84-92.

Jones, Thomas Frederick. "A Rhetorical Study of Black Songs: 1860-1930." Master's thesis, University of Georgia, Athens, 1973.

Keil, Charles. *Urban Blues*. Chicago: University of Chicago Press, 1966.

Korall, Burt. "The Music of Protest." *Saturday Review* 16 November 1968, 36-39.

Korson, George. *Coal Dust on the Fiddle*. Hatboro, PA: Folklore Associates, 1965.

Larson, Charles U. *Persuasion: Reception and Responsibility*. Belmont, CA: Wadsworth, 1989.

Lebacqz, Karen. *Professional Ethics*. Nashville, TN: Abingdon, 1985.

Lester, Julius. "Freedom Songs in the South." *Broadside* 39 (Feb. 7, 1964): 1-2.

Levine, Ellen, ed. *Freedom's Children: Young Civil Rights Activists Tell Their Own Stories*. New York: Avon, 1993.

Levine, Lawrence. *Black Culture and Black Consciousness*. New York: Oxford University Press, 1972.

Logue, Cal M. "Rhetorical Ridicule of Reconstruction Blacks." *Quarterly Journal of Speech* 62 (1976): 400-409.

Lomax, John A., and Alan Lomax. *Folk Song, U.S.A.* New York: New American Library, 1975.

Lovell, John, Jr. *Black Song: The Forge and the Flame*. New York: Macmillan, 1972.

Mills, Kay. *This Little Light of Mine: The Life of Fannie Lou Hamer*. New York: Dutton, 1993.

"Moment of History." *New Yorker* 27 March 1965, 37-39.

Oliver, Paul. *Songsters and Saints: Vocal Traditions on Race Records*. Cambridge: Cambridge University Press, 1984.

Payne, Charles M. *I've Got the Light of Freedom: The Organizing Tradition and the Mississippi Freedom Struggle*. Berkeley: University of California Press, 1995.

Perris, Arnold. *Music As Propaganda: Art To Persuade, Art To Control*. Westport, CT: Greenwood, 1985.

Putschogl, Gerhard. "Black Music--Key Force in Afro-American Culture: Archie Shepp on Oral Tradition and Black Culture." In *History and Tradition in Afro-American Culture*, edited by Gunter H. Lenz, 262-276. Frankfurt: Campus Verlag, 1984.

Raines, Howell. *My Soul Is Rested: Movement Days in the Deep South Remembered*. New York: Penguin, 1977.

Rawick, George P. *From Sundown to Sunup: The Making of the Black Community*. Westport, CN: Greenwood, 1972.

Reagon, Bernice Johnson. "In Our Hands: Thoughts on Black Music." *Sing Out!* November 1975, 1-2, 5.

———. "Songs of the Civil Rights Movement 1955-1965: A Study in Culture History." Ph.D. diss., Howard University, Washington, D.C., 1975.

———. Booklet accompanying three phonodiscs, *Voices of the Civil Rights Movement: Black American Freedom Songs, 1960-1966*. Washington: Smithsonian Institution, Program in Black American Culture, 1980.

———. "Let the Church Sing 'Freedom.'" *Black Music Research Journal* 7 (1987): 105-118.

Richmond, W. Edson. "The American Lyric Tradition." In *Our Living Traditions: An Introduction to American Folklore*, edited by Tristram P. Coffin, 94-107. New York: Basic, 1968.

Rustin, Bayard. *Strategies for Freedom: The Changing Patterns of Black Protest*. New York: Columbia University Press, 1976.

Scarborough, Dorothy. *On the Trail of Negro Folk-Songs*. Cambridge: Harvard University Press, 1925.

Seeger, Pete. "We Shall Overcome: The Complete Carnegie Hall Concert." Columbia C2K 45312, re-release, 1989.

Seeger, Pete, and Bob Reiser. *Everybody Says Freedom*. New York: W.W. Norton, 1989.

Sharp, Cecil. *English Folk Songs from the Southern Appalachians*. Volume 2. London: Oxford University Press, 1932.

Sherman, Robert. "Sing a Song of Freedom." In *The American Folk Scene: Dimensions of the Folksong Revival*, edited by David A. DeTurk and A. Poulin, Jr., 172-180. New York: Dell, 1967.

Sidran, Ben. *Black Talk*. New York: Holt, Rinehart & Winston, 1971.

Small, Christopher. *Music of the Common Tongue: Survival and Celebration in Afro-American Music.* New York: River Run Press, 1987.

Smith, Arthur L. *Rhetoric of Black Revolution.* Boston: Allyn and Bacon, 1969.

Stampp, Kenneth M. *The Peculiar Institution.* New York: Knopf, 1967.

Sutherland, Elizabeth, ed. *Letters from Mississippi.* New York: McGraw, 1965.

Taft-Kaufman, Jill. "Rhetorical Implications of Shakespeare's Changes in His Source Material for *Romeo and Juliet.*" In *Rhetorical Dimensions in Media: A Critical Casebook,* edited by Martin J. Medhurst and Thomas W. Benson, 344-363. Rev. printing. Dubuque, IA: Kendall/Hunt, 1984.

Turner, Ralph H. "Determinants of Social Movement Strategies." In *Human Nature and Collective Behavior,* edited by Tamotsu Shibutani, 145-164. Englewood Cliffs, NJ: Prentice-Hall, 1970.

Watters, Pat. *Down To Now: Reflections on the Southern Civil Rights Movement.* New York: Random, 1971.

Weisbrot, Robert. *Freedom Bound: A History of America's Civil Rights Movement.* New York: W.W. Norton, 1990.

White, E.E. "Solomon Stoddard's Theories of Persuasion." *Speech Monographs* 26 (1962): 235-259.

White, Newman I. *American Negro Folk-Songs.* Cambridge: Harvard University Press, 1928.

Williams, Juan. *Eyes on the Prize: America's Civil Rights Years, 1954-1965.* New York: Viking, 1987.

Work, John W. *American Negro Songs and Spirituals.* New York: Bonanza, 1940.

"Without These Songs." *Newsweek* 31 August 1964, 74.

Zinn, Howard. *The Southern Mystique.* New York: Knopf, 1964.

———. *SNCC: The New Abolitionists.* 2nd ed. Boston: Beacon, 1965.

Copyright Notices

Index